New Member
\# 1.38
.65
──────
\# 2.03.

John E Chappell
8 Oct 85

The Heights
of Courage

Memorial to the 77th Battalion in the Golan Heights

To my comrades-in-arms
and
To the bereaved parents

CONTENTS

FOREWORD

The history of battle is rich with examples in which the few have overcome the many, and in so doing defied the calculus of numbers that so distorts our ability to both predict battle outcomes beforehand and understand battle outcomes after the battle.

From the beginning, historians of all times have sought to capture the secret of why battles turn out as they do, all too frequently contradicting all expected outcomes. Successful attempts to do this are few indeed.

While the Yom Kippur War has had many chroniclers, none yet, in English, has described in true depth the "Face of Battle" in that war. The saga of Battalion 77 on the Golan Heights in 1973, a story with the code name of OZ [Courage] 77, appeared first in Hebrew not too long after the October War. Even then, reading a very sketchy early translation, one could not help but be gripped by the exciting and stark realism of the accounting. It was that excitement, and the realization that here was one of the most marvelous battle stories, as well as one of the most marvelously well-written battle stories of all times, that caused many readers of that early account to encourage that OZ 77 be translated into English.

Those who have fought will recognize this as a true story of battle, recounted by a small-unit commander. For here are the all too familiar and essential features all battles stamp on their participants: the confused, uncertain, ever-changing kaleidoscope of enemy and friendly locations, movements, situations; the unpredictable vagaries of human behavior under terrible stress; the ever-present specter of uncertainty and fear that deep down gnaw forever at battles' contestants; the essential and vital challenge of surviving to do what was decided on at the outset. All those and more are here—in the lines, between the lines.

Those who have studied battle applaud General Kahalani's unique skill at describing, without appearing to do so, battle's essential lessons: the vital need for coordination of all-arms warfare; the difficulties of reorganizing to continue to fight as losses occur; the ever-present struggle to rearm and refuel part of the force while another part fights on; the certain need for commanders to command from well forward, and the sure knowledge that as they do, casualties among them will be disproportionately high. All these and more besides are here—in the lines, between the lines.

Since the Yom Kippur War, General Kahalani and his friends have fought yet another war. When it is written, the history of that war—the War for Peace in Galilee—will show dramatically how well the battle lessons of the Yom Kippur War have been applied to improve battle concepts, tactics, organization, equipment and training in the IDF, especially in its Armored Corps.

However, in both wars, a decade apart, as in all of Israel's wars, as in the history of all battles, in the end the outcome was and will be in the hands of a few courageous men and their superb leaders who had trained themselves so very well in battle's difficult tasks that they prevailed despite sometimes desperate odds. While one espouses the eternal hope for peace, for an end to war, it is nonetheless essential to remember always that peace is a fragile commodity at best, and that it is quite likely that somewhere, sometime, once again, national goals, aspirations, aims—even national survival—will rest in the hands of a few courageous soldiers and their indomitable leaders who trained well in time of peace that they might fight and win in time of war. This is the legacy of the men of Courage 77 and their valorous leader.

Tampa, Florida   Donn A. Starry
March 1983   General, U.S. Army, Retired

PREFACE

The 1973 Yom Kippur War was essentially a tank war conducted under extremely adverse conditions. A series of errors on Israel's part had rendered the opening situation of the war highly unfavorable. The Israel Defense Forces (IDF) were thus obliged to employ inappropriate tactics during the first days of the hostilities.

Since the IDF did not mobilize in time, the enemy offensives in the north and south were consequently directed against a small standing force of regulars who fought against overwhelming odds. To make matters worse, Israeli troops were surprised by the sheer masses of modern weapons systems that the enemy employed against Israeli tanks and aircraft.

Given such circumstances, Israeli armor was forced to contain the enemy offensive by piecemeal counterattacks against large, well-organized forces—in direct contradiction to the principles of armored warfare. These attacks succeeded in breaking the enemy drives in both theaters of combat—but at great cost. The IDF Armored Corps paid with the lives of many of its best soldiers. Courage, daring and personal sacrifice were the legacy of all Armored Corpsmen from general down to private.

Use of inappropriate tactics is, of course, not a new phenomenon in the history of armored warfare. However, in the first days of the Yom Kippur War, the IDF employed poor tactics not for want of knowledge but out of lack of choice. Despite these constraints, the IDF Armored Corps succeeded in rallying and, in the course of the war, was able to revert back to proper tactics. Unlike the Armored Corps of other armies confronted by similarly unfortunate situations, the IDF Armored Corps was able to overcome these initial difficulties and not only save itself but the nation as well.

In the southern theater, the Armored Corps began to rally on
14 October. The Egyptians, who had planned the war with great
care, knew that it would be possible to achieve in-depth strategic
gains only by means of mobile, armored formations. However,
they were well aware of their own shortcomings and knew that
the IDF Armored Corps enjoyed a qualitative advantage over
Egyptian forces and that they stood no chance of defeating the
Israelis in mobile combat. The Egyptians therefore set for themselves more limited military objectives which could be attained
by non-mobile operations through the use of firm bases, sta-
tionary air defense dispositions, artillery and logistic support
bases on the western side of the Suez Canal.

On 14 October, it appeared to the Egyptians that the magni-
tude of their surprise offensive had knocked the Israeli forces
off balance. The Egyptians therefore decided to further profit
from their good fortune by "exploiting their initial success."
They committed armored formations to the eastern bank of the
Canal in an effort to reach the Mitleh-Gidi Pass line, in accor-
dance with plans that had been drawn up for such a contingency.

On that day, Israeli tanks destroyed approximately 300 Egyptian tanks. This blow constituted the turning point of the war
in the southern theater. The Egyptians' offensive came to an
end and was not to be renewed. The initiative now passed into
the hands of the Israelis, who took the offensive and forced the
Egyptians to maintain a defensive posture for the remainder of
the hostilities. Israeli armored divisions crossed the Suez Canal
and destroyed Egyptian layouts and surface-to-air missile bases.
They destroyed the Egyptian Third Army's rear logistic infra-
structure and then surrounded the Army itself, deploying along
the road to Cairo, thereby forcing Egypt to accept a cease-fire.

In the north, Israeli armor began to rally on 9 October. Avigdor
Kahalani's book is part of the story of how Israeli troops contained the Syrian offensive, launched a counteroffensive and
advanced toward Damascus, obliging the Syrians to request a
cease-fire.

This book is the story of an excellent brigade, from the commander himself down to the lowest-grade soldier, a brigade that,
along with other IDF units and formations, succeeded in de-

stroying most of the attacking Syrian troops and all Syrian tanks that had penetrated the Golan Heights.

In the future, the Armored Corps will continue to be the decisive element of IDF ground forces. It may well be that in future wars, Israeli troops will once again have to defeat vastly outnumbering enemy forces in offensives based on integrated armored formations. Such formations will be required to thrust deep into enemy territory. This is the real subject of Kahalani's book. Kahalani tells us how such warfare was conducted during the Yom Kippur War.

This is the first time in Israel that such a book has been written about armored warfare: a first-person account of a combatant describing the reality, fear and heroism of the battlefield. The uniqueness and strength of the book resides in that it graphically describes a situation often repeated in the annals of our military history. The Arabs fought a war in which they were ready to shed blood to further political goals, while Kahalani and his fellow soldiers fought for their own self-preservation and that of their nation. Israel exists by the grace of her dead and living heroes.

Kahalani and his comrades-in-arms have already fought three wars. The Yom Kippur War may not be the last one. The present account characterizes the spirit of the IDF Armored Corpsman, from Siman Tov Ganah, hero of the 1948 War of Independence (who had been decorated with the Medal of Valor, Israel's highest military decoration), to the author of this book (who has been decorated with the very same honor) and his fellow Armored Corpsmen who may again be called upon to form an iron wall protecting Israel until peace shall finally prevail.

1975   Major-General Israel Tal
           (From the Preface of the original Hebrew version.)

ACKNOWLEDGMENTS

I wish to express my deep gratitude to Louis Williams, the principal translator of the original, Hebrew, edition; to Marlin Levin, for editing the manuscript and for his guidance; to Richard Gabriel, for his vital assistance and advice in preparing the work for publication; to Norman Stahl of the Jewish Federation, for helping in its construction; and to Barbara Gallagher, who labored long and hard in typing the manuscript.

ABOUT THE AUTHOR

Brigadier-General Avigdor Kahalani was born on June 16, 1944, in Ness Ziona (Flag of Zion), a town in west-central Israel founded in 1883 and so named because it was there that the Jewish blue-white Star of David flag was first flown in the country. After completing elementary school in Ness Ziona and high school studies at ORT, a technical secondary school in Tel Aviv, he entered the Israel Defense Forces in 1962. He joined the Armored Corps, became a gunner on a Centurion tank, took a tank commanders' course and went on to complete officers' school.

General Kahalani served as a platoon leader and battalion operations officer, and in the 1967 Six-Day War, he commanded a company of M-48 Patton tanks. Badly wounded in the battle for El Arish, in northern Sinai, he was hospitalized for one year. He gradually returned to service in the Armored Corps, and in 1972, he finished a course in Israel's Command and Staff College. When the 1973 war broke out, he was in command of a battalion of Centurions.

After the war, he took charge of the Seventh Brigade. In 1978, he studied at the Command and General Staff College (CGSC) at Fort Leavenworth, Kansas. In 1980, he was promoted to the rank of brigadier-general and was given command of a division.

General Kahalani received the Distinguished Service Medal for his role in the Six-Day War, and the Medal of Valor, Israel's highest and rarely awarded military decoration, for supreme courage in the 1973 Yom Kippur War, the subject of this memoir.

The Heights of Courage originally appeared in Hebrew in 1975 under the title *OZ 77*, the designation of the author's battalion which fought on the Golan Heights in the 1973 war. The book was a best-seller and helped make Kahalani a household name in Israel. His heroic deeds in war have assured him a place in the folklore of modern Israel.

The author and his wife, Dalia, have three children, Dror, Vardit and Dotan.

INTRODUCTION

Ten years have passed since the outbreak of the Yom Kippur War, one of the most difficult, if not the most difficult, in the history of modern Israel.

Since 1973, many accounts have been written about the struggle but none from the vantage point of the men fighting in the line. It is from that aspect—from my own experiences and those of my comrades-in-arms—that I have written this memoir. In so doing, I have tried to shed light on the remarkable courage and skill these men displayed as they stopped the Syrian attempt to conquer the Golan Heights.

As I wrote the pages that follow, I had always before me the faces of the men with whom I fought side by side and, especially, of those who fell. It was important to me to communicate our emotions to the readers, particularly to the bereaved parents, widows and orphans, as we battled to keep the enemy at bay. I hoped that I could impart to the families some sense of their men's devotion to duty and of the price they were willing to pay to safeguard their nation and their people. Those on the home front have every right to feel proud of their fighting fathers, husbands and sons.

In focussing on these men, I could not deal at any length with the larger story of our division, brigade or 175 other battalions. Essentially, this is the story of one battalion at war. Nevertheless, it should in no way detract from the heroism shown by the men of these units.

Our brigade was well trained and was therefore well prepared for the war when it broke upon us. Thanks for that must go to the brigade commanding officer, Col. Avigdor "Yanosh" Ben-Gal.

I am grateful to those who granted me access to the taped recordings of battle conversations that went out over brigade net. Likewise, I am indebted to those men who were willing to recall for me their battlefront experiences and feelings—never an easy task. Without their help this book would not have been written.

Ness Ziona, Israel   Avigdor Kahalani
March 1983   Brigadier-General, IDF

THE SOLDIERS

Capt. Menahem Albert, Company Commander, "Zechar"
Capt. Shmuel Askarov, Deputy Battalion Commander
Cpl. Naomi Baharav, Secretary to Avigdor Kahalani
Lt.-Col. Haim Barak, Battalion Tank Commander
Lt. Achinoam Baruchin, Assistant Brigade Operations Officer
lst Sgt. Yisrael Barzilai, Tank Commander
lst Sgt. Amir Bashari, Tank Commander
Col. Avigdor "Yanosh" Ben-Gal, Brigade Commander
Lt.-Col. Yosef "Yossi" Ben-Hanan, Battalion Commander
Sgt. Ofer Ben-Neriya, Tank Commander
Col. Yitzhak Ben-Shoham, Brigade Commander
2nd Lt. Doron Biber, Platoon Leader
lst Sgt. Yoav Bluman, Tank Commander
Maj. Benjamin "Benzi" Carmeli, Company Commander, Six-
    Day War
Lt. Georgi Dani, Deputy Company Commander
Lt. Amihai "Ami" Doron, Deputy Company Commander
Capt. Menahem Dror, Company Commander
1st Sgt. David Edri, Tank Commander
Brig.-Gen. Rafael "Raful" Eitan, Division Commander
Lt.-Col. Ehud Elad, Battalion Commander, Six-Day War
Lt.-Gen. David "Dado" Elazar, IDF Chief of Staff
Lt.-Col. Yos Eldar, Mechanized Infantry Battalion Commander
2nd Lt. Boaz Eliav, Platoon Leader
Maj. Shalom Engle
Maj. Oded Erez, Battalion Commander
2nd Lt. Alex Eshel, M.D., Battalion Medical Officer
2nd Lt. Boaz Freedman, Platoon Leader
Maj. Arthur Gafni, Brigade Logistics Officer

Lt. Eli Geva, Company Commander
Col. Shmuel Gonen (Gorodish), 7th Brigade Commander, Six-
    Day War
1st Sgt. Zelig Haberman, Tank Commander
Capt. Yohanan Hasson, Logistics Officer
Maj.-Gen. Yitzhak "Haka" Hofi, Commander, Northern Com-
    mand
Cpl. Arnon Kahalani, Tank Mechanic, brother of Avigdor
Lt.-Col. Avigdor Kahalani, Commander, 77th Battalion, now
    Brigadier-General
Dalia Kahalani, wife of Avigdor
Dror Kahalani, son of Avigdor and Dalia
lst Sgt. Emanuel Kahalani, brother of Avigdor
Ruthi Kahalani, sister-in-law of Avigdor
Vardit Kahalani, daughter of Avigdor and Dalia
Cpl. "Kako," Jeep driver
Lt. Uri Kar-Shani, Commander, Reconnaisance Company
Lt.-Col. Amos Katz, Battalion Commander
Maj. Benjamin "Benny" Katzin, Brigade Operations Officer
Pvt. David Kilyon, Tank Gunner
2nd Lt. Shalom Kobi, Battalion Communications Officer
Capt. Eitan Kowli, Deputy Battalion Commander
Pvt. Yuval Kutchevsky, Kahalani's Tank Driver
Maj.-Gen. Dan Laner, Division Commander
Lt. Ephraim Laor, Company Commander, "Zilia"
Lt. Amnon Lavie, Company Commander, "Matress"
Capt. Amos Luria, Battalion Operations Officer
Capt. Ilan Maoz, Battalion Tank Officer
Maj. Yosef "Yossi" Melamed, Deputy Battalion Commander
Lt.-Col. Aryeh Mizrahi, Brigade Artillery Officer
Lt.-Col. Yair Nafshi, Battalion Commander
2nd Lt. Amos Nahum, Platoon Leader
Capt. Yonathan "Yoni" Netanyahu, Commander of Reconnais-
    ance Force
Lt. Avraham "Emmy" Palant (Killed at Entebbe in rescue of
    Israeli hostages, 7-4-76), Company Commander, "Houmous"
Lt. Gideon "Gidi" Peled, Battalion Operations Officer
Lt.-Col. Menahem Ratess, Battalion Commander
Maj. Haggai Regev, Brigade Operations Officer

Pvt. Avi Sandler, Tank Crewman
Lt. Ilan Shemaya, brother-in-law of Avigdor
Capt. Reuven Shemaya, brother-in-law of Avigdor
2nd Lt. Avinoam Shemesh, Platoon Leader
Lt. Avraham Snir, Battalion Artillery Support Officer
Capt. Shmuel Stolerov, Brigade Signals Officer
Lt. Yair Swet, "Vespa," Company Commander
Lt. Ofer Tabori, Platoon Leader
Maj. Yona Teren
2nd Lt. Noah Timienker, Platoon Leader
Pvt. Moshe Uliel, Tank Crewman
Capt. Adam Weiler, Company Commander, personal friend of
    Avigdor Kahalani
Maj. Gideon Weiler, brother of Adam, Deputy Battalion
    Commander
2nd Lt. Avi Yahav, Platoon Leader
Lt.-Col. David Yisraeli, Deputy Brigade Commander
Lt. Daniel Zafoni, Deputy Company Commander, Six-Day War
Capt. Meir Zamir, Company Commander, "Tiger"
1st Sgt. Moshe Zand, Company Sergeant-Major
2nd Lt. Yishai Zarhi, Platoon Leader
Lt. Eitan Zeiman, Platoon Leader

DISPOSITIONS AT "OPEN FIRE" 6 OCTOBER

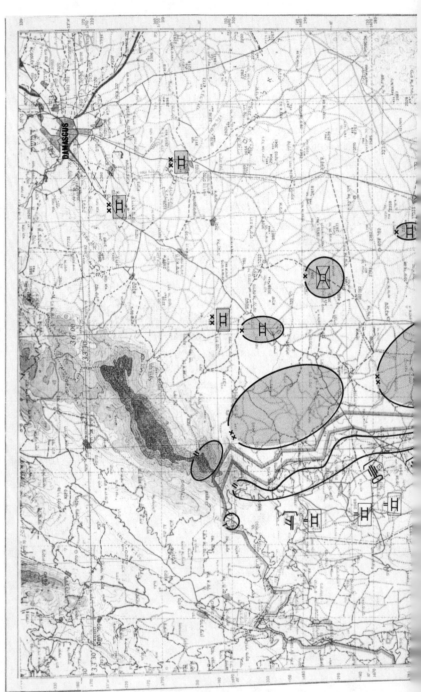

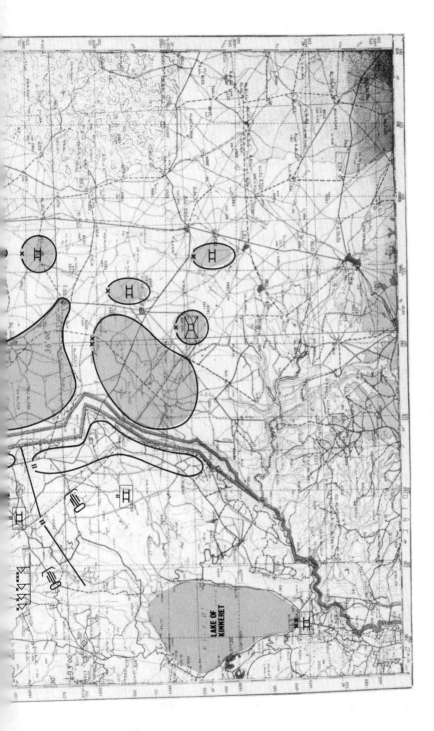

LAKE OF
KINNERET

CONTAINMENT AND COUNTER ATTACK IN THE GOLAN 6-10 OCTOBER

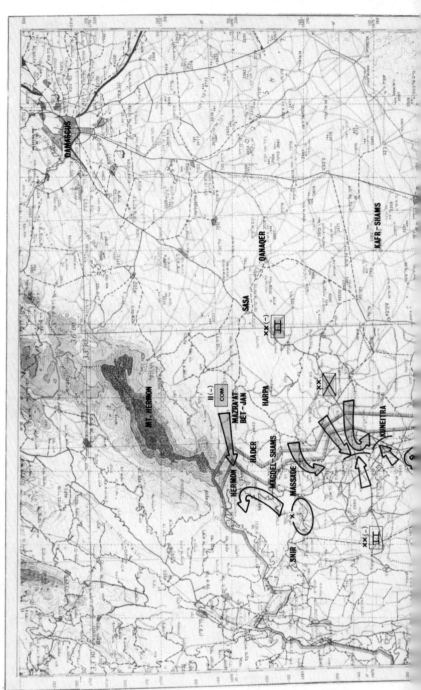

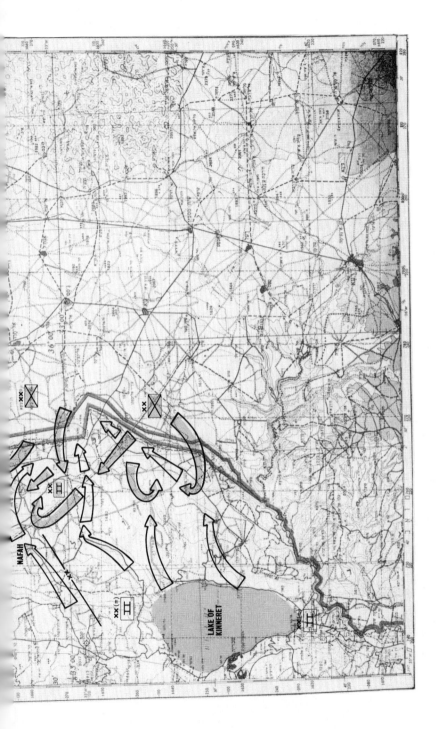

BREAKTHROUGH INTO SYRIAN GOLAN 11 – 24 OCTOBER

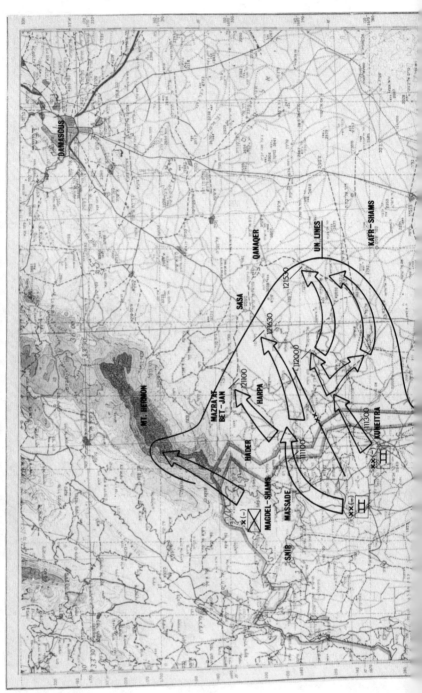

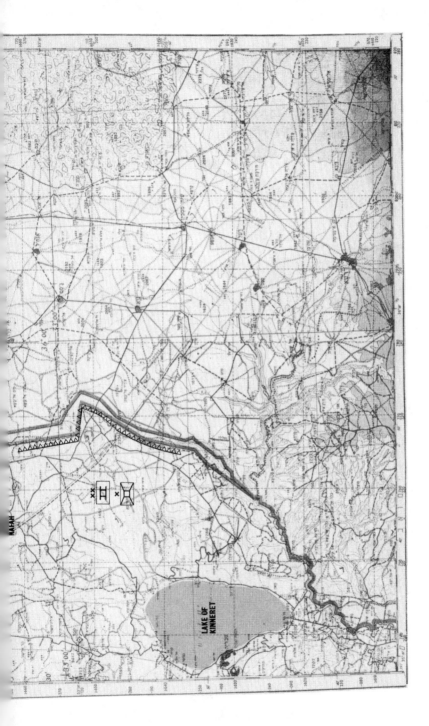

LAKE OF
KINNERET

The Heights
of Courage

1

SEPTEMBER 26, 1973   MORNING

I was on the roof, not feeling my best, when the phone rang. Tiles had to be replaced before the winter rains began, and my head throbbed from the aftereffects of last night's wedding party. My brother Emanuel had married Ruthi.

Dalia called me down. It was urgent, she said.

"Who is it?" I asked with some annoyance.

"Yanosh!"

What the devil could the brigade commander want now, on the eve of Jewish New Year. I clambered to the ground.

"Shalom," I said with some hesitation.

"Kahalani? This is Raeli. The brigade commander wants to tell you something." Yanosh would not call personally now unless. . . .

"What's going on?" I asked Raeli.

"It's getting lively. Hold on. I'm connecting you."

"Kahalani? What are you doing right now?"

"Fixing my roof. Why? Something happened?"

"Your battalion is on the alert." OZ 77,* under my command, was stationed deep inside Sinai. "Part of the battalion is moving north in a few minutes. A few companies for the time being."

"North?"

"Your duty officer has details. Nothing to worry about. Assemble your staff and report to Ben-Shoham. He'll supply tanks and tell you what you have to do."

"Something special up there?"

---

*OZ 77 is the Hebrew word for courage, valor. The number 77 is the numerical equivalent of the Hebrew letters of OZ.

"Yes, but not over the phone. You'll be under Ben-Shoham's command."

"Okay. No problem."

"I'll be up in the morning. You'll be representing the brigade till I get there."

As I put the receiver down, the questions in my mind were coming fast and furious: which companies, what equipment, where were all my officers, what was happening in the north— and when, dammit, would I finish repairing the tiles? But first, how was I to tell my wife that we would be apart for yet another holiday?

"Dalia, I'm going up north."

"When?"

"Now."

"How long for?"

"I don't know. The battalion is on its way. I'll phone my staff from here. Sounds like the Golan is warming up. Can you get my kit ready while I phone?" At least that would keep her mind off the inevitable questions—which I couldn't answer anyway.

My first call was to my deputy, Eitan. He promised to round up the others and call back before I left. Then to Emmy, commander of H Company, to tell him to head for the Golan and start arranging to requisition tanks and equipment; Ami Doron, his deputy, would bring up the company from the south. Next, the base in Sinai, though I knew I wouldn't find Menahem Albert—the duty officer. I had given him special permission to meet his relief, Yair Swet, at the airfield so he would still be able to get home for the holiday. But I spoke to Ami. He told me that he was closing up all the tanks (they had been opened for routine maintenance), was checking crews by the rosters, and was making sure that all the equipment was ready.

Swet phoned to say that he couldn't get down to the base. I told him that Menahem would stay on as duty officer. Then I had the unpleasant task of telling Menahem that I must have a company commander on the spot, even though his company was going north. Finally I had to reassure him that we wouldn't start a war without him. One of my pet dislikes was having to deliver that kind of message to a subordinate by telephone rather than in person.

Dalia was ready with my kit. The marathon on my newly installed phone was over.

"I was happy at the idea of being together for three whole days."

"So was I, but you must understand. . . ."

Whenever we had to part, the question always reverted to "understanding," but it didn't last long. Dalia was that rare woman—a soldier's wife who did understand. But there had been so few leaves from the sands of Sinai. . . .

Collecting Haim, my driver, we raced north along roads crammed with last-minute holiday eve traffic, past pedestrians in their holiday finery. Climbing the slopes to Golan, the scene changed abruptly. The traffic was military, and the camps by the roadside were going about workday routines at full strength despite the approach of Rosh Hashana, the Jewish New Year.

2

SEPTEMBER 26, 1973 AFTERNOON

It was only three days since my last trip up to the Golan Heights. Yanosh must have had a premonition about the holiday season, for he brought all the brigade staff and battalion commanders on a familiarization tour, though for me it had been more like a refresher. I spent the holidays of 1972 on this sector, expecting a Syrian retaliation following a police action inside Lebanon.

Ben Shoham wasn't in his office when I arrived, but I did find David Yisraeli, his deputy. David had been chief instructor at Armor School when I was commander of the gunnery section. My first posting after command and Staff College had been as deputy battalion commander under David, then as battalion commander when he moved up to the second spot in the brigade. It wasn't easy working with him, because my inexperience had led me into encroaching on his command prerogatives. Delicately but firmly, David put me in my place. From then on we got along well, until finally he delegated the battalion staff work to me—and told me afterwards that he had never believed himself capable of doing that with anyone.

David greeted me like a long lost friend, then filled me in on the details; my battalion would serve as the brigade tactical counterattack force. Telling me where to draw tanks and equipment, he said that we must be ready for anything by dawn next day. Ben-Shoham was inspecting the line, so I went to look over the supply base while waiting for my officers to arrive, after agreeing to meet the brigade commander later. The quartermaster told me that their Centurions had been checked out by armorers only a week before and, sure enough, everything seemed in tip-top condition. My mind at rest on that score, I went on to my meeting with Ben-Shoham.

We met on the road. Climbing down from his Jeep, he walked over to greet me, asking first of all about Dalia.

"Kahalani, you're drawing tanks from my emergency stores, and all the quartermaster crews are at your service. The Syrians are massing tanks and artillery, and I want you organized quickly."

"No problem. Do we have anything on their intentions?"

"Assumptions that they'll try a bombardment, or perhaps invest a forward position on the line. Some people are suggesting that they want a chunk of Golan."

"What's my job?"

"Set up at Nafah crossroads and be ready to make counterstrikes wherever necessary. There is a problem. Much as I would like to put you in the camp at the crossroads, the buildings are occupied by an infantry company commander's course. I'm trying to get them out, but perhaps you should take a look at the possibilities at Sindiana. One other request.... We put the tanks in new sheds not long ago. Try not to mess up the asphalt floors."

"Right. I'll watch them."

"I know it's ridiculous if we do have a war, but these things usually don't end that way, and a lot of money has been spent...."

Strange the things a man remembers at times like these. I was thinking about company commanders' course at Armor School. Ben-Shoham commanded my course. It was during the War of Attrition. On the morning I heard that Adam Weiler, who was like a brother to me, had fallen in action, I asked Ben-Shoham for leave to attend the funeral. He said he would think about it, and I meanwhile arranged to be among the pallbearers. Hearing about it, he reprimanded me—in a towering rage—for going behind his back and taking things for granted. We stopped talking to each other. Some time later, on a field exercise, he came over.

"Kahalani, you still furious with me?"

"No."

"I read in *Ma'Ariv* [an Israeli newspaper] about your special relationship with Adam. I didn't know. I'm truly sorry."

My men began to arrive. Eitan took charge of tank allocation

to the crews—as they arrived. Meanwhile, I split my two companies and the few extra crews from First Battalion into three,
under Eli Geva—who had come from First—Yair Swet and Emmy
Palant. I ordered Emmy to make one tank, and his best crew,
available to me. His face soured at the suggestion that he might
give me anything but the best. Then I drove out with the brigade
reconnaissance officer to look over the tank paths around Nafah
crossroads and was again warned about sensitivities over Golan
roads—this time, about not taking tracked vehicles across the
roads except on concrete aprons. We also looked at Sindiana,
but there was neither water nor shade, and we could be expected
to spend a few days on full alert.

Returning to brigade, I told Ben-Shoham that we weren't
spoiled, having come from Sinai, but Nafah crossroads would
be preferable. Still, the infantry was there, and much as he was
leaning in my direction, he couldn't decide. Finally, David and
I went to have a look at the camp, to try to see when the infantry
intended to move. We found a sergeant-major who held out
faint hopes of our prayer being answered. There was nothing
for it but to tell Ben-Shoham that we would take Sindiana. He
asked me to wait while a female clerk got the commanding
general on the line.

"General, shalom, Ben-Shoham speaking. Kahalani is here
with me. We have a problem. You remember we spoke about
his setting up at the crossroads. Well, there's an infantry course
in residence. Is there any way of getting them out of there?"

Ben Shoham listened intently, then answered some inaudible
question.

"In about half an hour. Thank you, General."

Hanging up the receiver, he turned to me.

"We've got a better solution. Stay right where you are—at the
stores. The infantry will be gone in two or three days."

"Fine. You're going to a lot of trouble."

"I want you to feel at home, Kahalani."

It was getting dark when I returned to battalion to find that
Yair, Geva and Emmy had taken care of the men as they disem-
barked from the buses. The place now had the air of organized
chaos that accompanies fighting men organizing for business.
The technical teams were arranging their tools. Medical corps-

men were busy with the boxes that made up a battalion field reception station. The signallers were sorting out their equipment. Because of the three-company split, we had to move tanks to make room for stacks of ammunition between them. As they started to roll, a quartermaster came running.

"Sir, sorry to bother you, but there's an urgent problem."

I waited, knowing full well what he was going to say.

"Your men are moving from shed to shed. They'll churn up the whole camp—and it isn't necessary...."

"Hold it. Calm down. What's your name?"

"Willie, sir."

"Well, Willie, you organized the tanks for your convenience, but I can't allow my companies to be spread all over the place, so let's take a look at how we can do it without ruining anything, okay?"

"But why move them? They're only loading ammunition and fixing barrels."

"Willie, I told you they will move, and I mean it. But why don't you guide them?"

With some chagrin, we agreed. Again I had to admire the devotion these men had for their equipment, and I marveled at how much personal direction Ben-Shoham and David invested in them to foster it!

My crews were joined by raw recruits from Golani Brigade. They helped remove shells from the crates—and they were welcome indeed. Then I instructed the men to zero gunsights, using a star or a distant light as their reference. I wanted to be sure we would be ready to move by morning. Satisfied with the work in progress, I phoned Yanosh to report.

"Kahalani, I want you to get some sleep. Leave the rest to Eitan. You have to be wide awake tomorrow."

He was right. Still tired from the wedding celebration, I needed the sleep, but I also had to set an example. I watched from the sidelines. Eitan was supervising the loading of ammunition and checking off lists of equipment with each crew. The armorer and his men were inspecting the tanks. My signals officer was making sure that the instruments were properly installed and tuned to the right frequencies—though he could only do dry runs: we were under orders to preserve radio silence. The battalion doctor was turning his half-track into a mobile hospital—lashing equipment boxes, loading stretchers and inspecting the personal kits of his orderlies.

At 0300 hours, sure that everything was in competent hands, I told Eitan that I was turning in and would relieve him in the morning. Meanwhile, he was to start engines and boresight the gunsights at dawn.

3

SEPTEMBER 27, 1973

I awoke before 0600 hours. Glancing out the window, I saw Yanosh's car, and was surprised that no one had called me. Eitan came in, clean-shaven and washed.

"Good morning," he said with a broad smile.

"Good morning. Whose car is that?" I asked—though I knew the answer.

"Brigade commander. He arrived a half hour ago."

"Why didn't you wake me?"

"He didn't want me to," he replied in a mischievous tone. "You see, he is concerned about you."

"What about the tanks?"

"Fully equipped, and all ammunition stowed. There are a few problems, but I'll solve them during the morning."

"Engines?"

"All warmed up. Gidi [battalion operations officer] has gone off to boresight gunsights, but it isn't easy. The terrain doesn't allow more than a thousand yards."

"It's more than enough."

I dressed quickly and went out to join Yanosh, who also looked tired.

"Good morning, Kahalani. How are things?"

"As you can see, we're ready to move."

"Eitan told me that you were made welcome."

"Yes. We have a few things to finish, but otherwise. . . ."

"What did Ben-Shoham tell you?"

"We're the brigade reserve for counterattack."

"Fine," he smiled. "Do you remember two weeks back I told you to be prepared for a move up here for the holidays?"

"Yes. I didn't take you seriously, but now I'm beginning to wonder. How did you know?"

"Instinct. But you'll see, the whole brigade will be here within the week."

"You know something?"

"Nobody's told me, but remember my words! What are you going to do today?"

"I'm taking the company commanders over the sector and the approach routes."

"Take the platoon officers as well! I'll go and have a talk with Ben-Shoham. Join me there afterwards and we'll go over the area together. Incidentally, I've brought Shalom, my signals officer, with me. He can help your signals officer."

We had a quick cup of coffee together with my staff officers, then Yanosh left to see Ben-Shoham.

Yanosh had been brigade commander for little more than a year. A tall man with a limp caused by a fall from a tank turret, he expected a great deal and used unorthodox methods to achieve results. Administration didn't interest him—performance was everything. Perhaps as a trademark, he used to let his hair grow wild, but has taken to getting it cut since he assumed command of the brigade.

After my tour with the company commanders, Yanosh and I went over the sector, examining every passable track and firing position, listening to a briefing from brigade intelligence on enemy dispositions, and determining where the battalion would stand. Yanosh went into every detail, even ordering preparation of range-finding cards for each position so we wouldn't need to waste ranging shots. At each forward post on the line, we received a situation report from the men. There was no noticeable activity. If they were massing, then it was deeper inside Syria.

Towards evening Yanosh and his officers left Golan, and I drove over to an orders group at Ben-Shoham's headquarters. After a briefing from Ben-Shoham and an assessment of forces on our sector from his operations officer, the brigade commander shared his assumptions with us.

"The Syrians have three options. They can try to take Quneitra or Tel Faras and so regain some of their self-respect. They can bombard the whole of Golan and help the terrorists. Third, and the least likely to my mind, they can try to take the Heights. I would opt for them trying the second approach—but I know that Yanosh doesn't agree," he added, looking at me and Ilan, Yanosh's intelligence officer, who had stayed on for the night.

Next up was the brigade intelligence officer—Ben-Shoham's this time—with the happy news that the Syrians had concentrated 800 tanks and 150 artillery batteries on the first line. That earned him some gasps of astonishment. We all knew how thin we were on the ground. The tanks didn't worry me much. They couldn't mass the lot in one place in case we hit them, and if they wanted to come at us—it could only be on a narrow sector. I asked what force he thought they would use if they decided to attack.

"Up to a division."

That would be about 250 tanks, and we were only one sector.

On the way back to battalion, I used the Jeep radio to alert my company commanders for an orders group with me. By the time I arrived, they were waiting in our improvised office. I quickly ran through the main points made at Ben-Shoham's briefing, then added my own assumptions on the points at which the Syrians would likely attack. Pointing out that we might have to split into two forces, and that orders would be given on the move, I stressed that we would spend every available moment learning the terrain.

"Now, where do you think we should stage armor against armor battles if we have to block them?"

"We don't let them cross the frontier," Yair offered. "The battle should be on their ground."

"Anyone think differently?"

"We must not let them cross the anti-tank ditch, otherwise we won't be using it properly and we'll have to stand on the ramps."

"Yes, I think that's about it. But remember, we won't be moving into any sector before there's a breakthrough and we know the main direction of the Syrian thrust. By then we may have to fight in our territory. We'll try to deploy above the anti-tank ditch, but we must be prepared for the other possibility."

Using a map, I picked out the likely points on each sector and discussed the best places to contain any breakthrough at those

points. Finally I asked who was familiar with Bustar Ridge, adding that I believed the Syrians would try to use Quneitra as their
springboard. The town was important to them psychologically.
If that was their route, then Bustar Ridge would be vital. The
meeting closed with my instructing Eitan to prepare armored
personnel carriers (APCs) for our tour of the area the next day.
We would be checking every track and possible firing position.
That done, we broke up to get a night's rest.

4

SEPTEMBER 28, 1973

We started out at dawn, with the intention of each company commander going to look at his own immediate sector, but on the way, I received an order to report to brigade headquarters for instructions regarding reconnaisance. I halted our cavalcade in the brigade area and went in to see Benny, the brigade operations officer. He gave me details of the roads near the frontier, and told me the limitations on traffic across the Golan Heights. Then he said I was free to send some of my officers home on leave. I decided on Eitan and Emmy, but Eitan thought I should go first. Finally he agreed, on condition that he leave only after our tour of the forward lines. He went off with Yair and Geva, while Emmy, Ilan—my intelligence officer—and I drove onto the northern sector.

Once we had an idea of what could and should be done in each area, all the battalion officers and tank commanders were given the same tour. When that was done, I packed Ami off to spend a day at home with his wife of a few months' standing. Then, having discovered a swimming pool hidden among the trees near our camp, I let the boys go, company by company, making sure that each group was accompanied by a vehicle with radio.

The rest of us carried on with the work of preparing the battalion for any eventuality.

5

SEPTEMBER 29, 1973

The day started with problems. It was Saturday, the Sabbath, but the men were on their feet at dawn as usual to carry out maintenance preparatory to a move—in case it was necessary. As I walked around the tanks, I noted that Yair and Geva were not with their men, and the fact was evident in the casual way in which the work was being done. I summoned them to me, and they came still wiping the sleep from their eyes. Geva's shirt was hanging out, and he didn't salute—a small gesture of military discipline that I insisted on every morning.

What followed was a somewhat rebellious argument about why company commanders didn't need to be present during the early morning chores. Finally I found out that Geva was annoyed because I had sent Emmy on furlough without consulting all the company commanders. There was nothing to do but tell him, quietly and firmly, that in my battalion, my orders were carried out; what he did in his own battalion, his commander permitting, had no bearing on the discipline that I maintained.

Our somewhat discordant session came to an end when Emmy came back from leave and took me aside to say that the gesture was appreciated. I returned to my room and sat on my bed in a foul mood, which only softened when Kako, my driver, brought me sandwiches and strong black coffee. Then Eitan walked in. Sensing something was wrong, he got the story out of me and told me that Geva's behavior pattern was the same everywhere. We checked off a few items together, then I took off for home, driving down the Jordan Valley to pick up Dalia from her parents' home in Jerusalem.

Since it was a holiday weekend, the whole family was there,

including Reuven, Dalia's twin brother, who was serving as a captain in intelligence. We didn't stay long because my own parents were giving a party for my brother Emanuel and his wife of less than a week.

Emanuel greeted me on the balcony outside the house.

"Sir," he said, saluting with perfect precision, "you're late."

"You couldn't wait?"

"I ordered them to, but there's no discipline here. They all went home."

"I don't know how you got to be a top sergeant if you can't control a few civilians."

Emanuel was obviously a little bit the worse for drink—no great achievement in his case, since one glass made him tipsy—but he turned serious for a moment.

"Avi, what's all this about you being on alert on Golan?"

"It's hot up there, and somebody has to defend you," I grinned.

"Do the Syrians want another war?"

"Nothing's clear yet. How was the honeymoon? Tell me, Ruthi, is he a good husband?"

"Right now he's a drunk husband."

"Drunk. I'll show you who's drunk," he yelled, swinging her over his shoulder and dancing around the balcony.

My father came out to join us.

"Well, Avi, that alert was heaven sent. It's all because you intended to work on your roof on a holiday."

I knew he hadn't liked the idea of me profaning the New Year, but now he assured me that he would do a few rows of tiles every day after work; I needn't worry about it.

Late that night Eitan phoned to say that Yanosh wanted him back at base to complete the battalion stocktaking, which was part of a brigade-wide routine, but which had now become even more urgent. We agreed to meet at Rosh Pina Airport in the morning.

6

SEPTEMBER 30, 1973

As I left the plane at Rosh Pina, I bumped into General Yitzhak Hofi, O/C Northern Command, walking to a Piper Cub.

"Kahalani, how are you?"

"Fine, thank you, sir. You know that I'm a guest in your sector?" I said.

"Sure I do. We moved your battalion this morning."

"What? Where to?"

"Don't worry. They're already back. There was news, so we stepped up the alert, but it's all okay for the moment."

General Hofi looked troubled.

"I see it's impossible to go home."

The general smiled, then promised to visit the battalion.

I met Eitan in the terminal building.

"Any special problems?" I asked.

"Yes. The camp gate is too narrow to allow free tank movement, and the area where we deployed was rocky—almost impossible to maneuver. Then you have to decide when to activate the radios. We have no instructions from brigade on that."

"Okay. I want you to call me from battalion. Make sure that the other companies are fully organized."

Eitan returned to Sinai, where the battalion base was located, and Kako drove me up to the Golan Heights. At the camp, I found Menahem, commander of G Company, who had come up to relieve Yair. Geva also left when Zamir came to replace him. I briefed both of them and packed them off on a tour of the forward positions.

OCTOBER 1, 1973

Now I had the whole battalion. Yair and Amnon arrived with their companies at full strength, and Eitan came with them. There was a problem: four companies and five company commanders. Not relishing the idea, I called in Amnon and told him that I would have to break up his company since he was lowest in seniority—but I wanted him to take over a small independent force made up of his tank, and Eitan's and Noah's platoons, attached to me. He would work with me. He obviously wasn't happy about breaking up his unit, but he took it in a good spirit.

The tanks that Yair and Amnon received were not as trim as the ones from Ben-Shoham's emergency stores—but we now had numbers, and that was a good feeling. Two more companies increased our options, though I didn't have a premonition of imminent war.

I set out on a tour of inspection and found my brother Arnon in Amnon's company. Arnon had just completed Ordnance Corps School. He was posted to a Centurion workshop in the center of the country, and he didn't like the idea. He had pressured me to get him down to Sinai.

Usually, in military surroundings, we avoided each other. But now Arnon wanted to know what was happening.

"What's up, Avi? We hear the Syrians mean business."

"Don't worry. What do you hear from home?" I asked.

"Emanuel and Ruthi have gone on a honeymoon."

"Do you have all the equipment you need?" I asked.

"Yep."

We exchanged a few more remarks. He went back to repairing a tank and I left.

OCTOBER 2, 1973

Yanosh appeared together with Haggai Regev, the brigade operations officer. He wanted to tour the line, but I preferred to do it together with my company commanders later in the day. We agreed to meet over lunch at Ben-Shoham's headquarters. Ben-Shoham laid on a meal that was most impressive, apparently trying to convince us of the culinary advantages of being in his brigade. I suggested to Yanosh that we should learn from the example.

After lunch we strolled over to the base swimming pool. I stripped and jumped in but couldn't convince any of the others to take the plunge. They were right. The water was freezing.

As Yanosh left, I sensed that he was uneasy at the thought of not being with us if something was going to happen. One thing we had done was to plan our training schedules for the week following Yom Kippur—the Day of Atonement—which this year fell on October 6. I was to arrange a model field exercise, to be observed by all the brigade officers. It was Yanosh's idea. He wanted to check the brigade's combat techniques. Nevertheless, he was still sure that war would interrupt the plan. So he ordered Ilan to prepare ample maps of the Golan Heights for the entire brigade in case they would all be brought up north.

In the evening, I met General Hofi and Ben-Shoham. Hofi showed me a map of the planned road network and explained that the present system was too poor to allow tanks the right-of-way on asphalt surfaces. There had also been too many fatal road accidents recently. I argued that if war did come, any of us who had to stick to dirt tracks wouldn't reach the key points in time.

"Listen," said Ben-Shoham, "we're still not at war. In any event, how much time will you lose by taking the dirt paths?"

I dropped the issue, feeling that time would tell.

9

OCTOBER 3 AND 4, 1973

I was called to David, the deputy brigade commander, in the morning to hear that we would be moving to Nafah the next day. Not because anything special had happened, but because of an earlier decision to place us in the central Golan.

There followed a long session in which he chewed me out for not requesting all the creature comforts that the brigade could, and would, supply. I said that it didn't seem right to fuss over a few days. David insisted that we weren't in the desert, that these were permanent bases, so I agreed to submit a list.

"The engineers will set up showers and field toilets for you," he said.

"Why not my own personal shower?" I joked.

That evening I assembled the battalion and lectured them on the Syrian border situation. The response was good. They understood why we were on the alert. We ended the day with an entertainment troupe laid on by Northern Command.

The next day at noon, we moved into Nafah Camp. Everything was organized quickly. Battalion headquarters moved into a big building that provided offices and sleeping quarters for the staff, the company commanders and the Women's Corps clerks who had come up to Golan with us.

That evening I went home to a wedding of an old school friend and arrived in the middle of the celebration, still in my army fatigues. My friends were surprised that I was on Golan while everything was so quiet. We didn't talk much about it. After all, it would soon pass, as alerts usually did.

OCTOBER 5, 1973

Up at dawn, I put a few more rows of tiles on the roof, with Dalia helping me. Then, while Ness Ziona was visibly preparing for the fast of Yom Kippur, I parted from our son Dror, who had just entered first grade, from our eighteen-month-old daughter, Vardit, and from Dalia. At 0800 hours, I was on my way back to Golan.

Eitan greeted me with the news that the whole brigade was moving up from Beersheba and would be on the Heights by evening. Apart from that, Yanosh wanted to see me at noon. I phoned Ben-Shoham, who said the line was being reinforced because the Syrians were up to something.

The battalion was preparing for Yom Kippur, and food was being distributed to those soldiers who wouldn't be fasting. Meanwhile, I was informed that the Northern Command chaplain wanted to spend the fast with us. I wasn't exactly delighted. The situation might require vehicle movements and other chores, and a rabbi on the spot would inhibit us. After the brigade chaplain assured me that there would be no friction on that count, we went together to choose a site for the synagogue services. Together with him, I made the rounds, wishing my men "well over the fast" and repeating that I hoped the synagogue would be full.

Yanosh's driver arrived to take me to a meeting. I found the brigade commander in a cheerful mood. The commanding general was in the area—somewhat unusual on Yom Kippur. Together with his staff officers, we settled down to study the map. Yanosh pinpointed the location of the other battalions.

"When Haim arrives, he'll go to Sindiana. Yos and Ratess will be near Nafah."

"Why not put Ratess at the crossroads near Forward Position Seven?"

"Ben-Shoham has a force there."

"Yes. Roughly a company—and they won't bother Ratess. He can use the buildings there and have good access to Quneitra."

"Good idea. I'll check it out with Ben-Shoham immediately."

Yanosh vanished into a nearby office, returning a few minutes later to confirm that Ben-Shoham had accepted my idea and would withdraw his own company.

"Kahalani. I want you to stay put. I intend to have your battalion returned to my command."

"When?"

"Tomorrow morning. I have to discuss it with the general."

"At the moment I am attached to Ben-Shoham, and I wouldn't like friction. But I'll be waiting to hear."

"Agreed. Until you hear otherwise, you are under Ben-Shoham. Meanwhile, coordinate frequencies with brigade signals, so that you'll be ready if, as and when. What's new in the battalion?"

I reported that all was ready, then invited Yanosh to spend the night with us. But he begged off.

"In your brigade people get hepatitis from the chow, and that's all I need!"

"You and your fears!" I replied. "We had one case of jaundice a few months previous, and Yanosh doesn't let me forget it."

I returned to battalion and called all the officers in for a briefing. I told them that the entire brigade was moving up tonight. Then we went over the rosters, crew by crew, checking equipment details, ensuring that everything was as ready as it ever would be. While we pored over lists, under the light of a 24-volt lamp, our men were praying in the synagogue next door.

"A large number of tanks will be arriving here during the night. I want a staff officer on duty all night to report to the brigade commander on the location of all vehicles, and where they are headed. The operations officer will place flare markers on the road. Remember, the brigade had one night in which to complete what we did in a number of days. From tomorrow morning we may—I repeat, may—be returning to brigade, so be prepared to switch frequencies on your radios, and remember the call signs: Yair—'Vespa'; Menahem—'Zechar'; Emmy— 'Houmus'; Amnon—'Matress'; Zamir—'Tiger'; the battalion net— 'Policeman.' Doctor, is your half-track ready?"

"There was a small hitch. It's been fixed."

"Eitan, do you have anything to add?"

"Yes, anyone who hasn't drawn seventy-two-hour battle rations should do so tonight. Apart from that, what about traffic tomorrow?"

It was a good point. After all, it was the Day of Atonement. I confirmed that nothing would move, apart from the water wagon and one command Jeep. When the officers split up, I called Gidi, my operations officer, to take a look at our tank. Everything was in working order, exactly as it had been when we tried it out a few days before. One last foot tour of the battalion lines, then I lay down to sleep, confident that Eitan had everything in good order.

I was awakened at midnight, as I had requested, and drove over to Yanosh's headquarters across the camp. He told me that Haim's battalion was almost fully equipped. Ratess would be arriving in the morning and would take his tanks straight to the place I had suggested. Then we talked about the need to split tanks off from each battalion to support Yos, who only had APCs.

"Kahalani, are you completely ready? We're going to have a serious war here."

The word *war* sent a chill down my spine. I knew what it meant. I also knew about 800 tanks and 150 artillery batteries on the Syrian frontline.

The battalion lines were quiet. It was 0200 hours on the Day of Atonement. Apart from the team directing brigade traffic on the road, all were sleeping deeply and peacefully.

OCTOBER 6, 1973—
DAY OF ATONEMENT

At dawn the hum of tank engines awakened me. The crews were carrying out maintenance preparatory to moving. After a quick turn around the camp, I went back to bed to doze for a while.

"Avigdor!"

I opened my eyes to find Gideon Weiler standing by my bed.

"What are you doing here?"

"Came to see you."

"So I see. What unit are you with?"

"I'm Ratess' deputy battalion commander. I've brought up the men from Armor School."

"Deputy battalion commander? Congratulations. How are things at home?"

"My parents are recovering. I'm living with them—in the same building, floor below."

"With Danny?"

"Yes."

I knew Gideon, Adam Weiler's brother, from my visits to the family home. Ever since Adam was killed in the War of Attrition, his family and comrades had been collecting material for the archives of a man who was so special to all of us—and this, together with the annual memorial meetings, had brought me very close to the family.

"When are you going to be a father, Gideon?"

"Few more months. How are Dror and Dalia?"

"Fine. Come and visit. There are a lot of changes. I'm building."

"It's a promise. Now I'm going to see what's going on with our tanks. I'll be back later."

At 0800 hours, a team of quartermaster officers came to find out what we needed for a prolonged stay. I got beds and mat-tresses for all the men, and was promised showers, latrines, mobile electric power equipment for the tents and a few other things. Towards the end of my session with them, Yanosh phoned. He wanted me to convene all the battalion and company commanders of the brigade for a briefing in my office. Urgent!

Lieutenant-Colonel Ratess turned up in a clean and pressed dress uniform; paratroop wings and campaign ribbons decorat-ing his broad chest, tank insignia pinned to his shirt pocket and beret neatly rolled under a shoulder epaulette. He was a first-rate and experienced professional and had proven himself in command of the top-level courses at Armor School. I had served as loader/radioman in his tank when he commanded a company. We respected him—and feared him. Now he was slated to be brigade commander of a standing army brigade, and instructors of his own rank willingly took orders from him. Ratess, a man who knew how and when to enjoy life and when to be serious, had become a concept in the Armored Corps.

He grinned, showing a row of shining white teeth, and greeted us. Haim and Yos, the other battalion commanders, arrived with him, and we all sat around a plank table, the kind generally used in mess halls. The room—my office—had openings for windows, but no frames or glass. The walls were covered with all the evidence of military inhabitants: slogans, paintings and miscellaneous graffiti. I hung a large-scale map of Golan, marked with all the main axes to the different sectors. My battalion was organized and ready.

I greeted Yanosh outside and escorted him into the room as all the officers rose to their feet. Yanosh didn't like military ceremonial but, as brigade commander, he paid particular at-tention to the necessary trappings.

"Be seated. We haven't got much time. Kahalani, who's here, and what's the state of the tanks?"

"My five company commanders and my deputy are present, and all the tanks are deployed under nets in my area."

"Haim?" Yanosh sounded impatient.

"Two company commanders present. The third is on his way with the last five tanks. I expect them within the hour."

"Are you already at Sindiana?"

"Yes. My command company is there with orders on how to deploy."

"Yos?"

"My reconnaissance company, with its APCs, has arrived. A few APCs are on their way here. I'll be ready within two hours."

Yos' unit was only APCs. I expected him to demand tanks, but he remained silent.

"Where are your company commanders?"

"Still on their way here. They will arrive with the last of the vehicles."

"No good. I want them here immediately. Leave one of your platoon commanders to supervise the APCs. Are you at Waset Junction?"

"Yes. I moved into the houses south of the crossing."

"Ratess?"

"My force is made up of maintenance people and instructors from Armor School. I'm short three tanks."

Yanosh nodded, and Ratess continued.

"Two of my company commanders are present. The third will arrive shortly. The last tanks will be here in an hour, and will go to Waset Junction. I haven't been there yet, but my deputy—Gideon—is in charge on the spot."

"Good. Now let's get down to business. Gentlemen, war will start today."

All eyes were on him. We thought he was pulling our leg, but his face was dead serious. The room was hushed.

"Yes, just what you heard. There will be war today, coordinated between Syria and Egypt. We don't yet know the precise hour, but it will start this afternoon or evening. This is verified information from top sources. I can't go into more detail because of security."

As one man, we looked at our watches: it was nearly 10:00.

"Now," Yanosh cracked the silence, "I want you to note the following...."

Out came our notebooks while whispered comments greeted the brigade commander's bombshell.

"These are the things that must be done. All equipment lashed to the tanks. All crews and vehicles ready for immediate move, the men in coveralls. Check machine guns. Zero sights and adjust barrels. Check firing circuits in the tanks. All ammunition is to be stowed properly and panels lashed in place on the tanks."

Some technical details were raised and resolved, then Yanosh asked, "Anyone doesn't know the Heights?"

"I don't," said Haim.

Two of Ratess' company commanders also raised their hands.

"Ratess, I gather that you haven't been up here recently?"

"A long time ago."

"In that case, we'll attach somebody to you who is familiar with the area."

"Sir, my reconnaissance plan is ready," observed Haggai, brigade operations officer. "I'll go with Haim from Sindiana toward the southern sector. Zamir will join Yos on the central and northern tour, and Eli Geva will drive with Ratess."

Yanosh considered it for a moment.

"Alright. Just check communications before you move."

Turning to his signals officer, he added, "Give them call signs, Shalom."

"They can use Kahalani's net and number. We mustn't open new nets."

"Any questions?"

None.

"Battalion commanders report to me at 14:00."

We split up. I had a word with my company commanders before they rejoined their men. I ordered them to stop the Yom Kippur fast and close the synagogue so that every man would be in place. I confirmed the radio frequencies, then turned back into the room. Yanosh was still seated.

"So, it's serious this time?"

"Yes, very serious, Kahalani. I want everything done speedily—and well."

"It will be."

"The families of the Russians in Cairo and Damascus began to leave for home yesterday. That's a sure sign they're planning to do something big. Kahalani, remember, everything is developing according to my appraisal."

"I still hope you're wrong."

"I'm building a great deal on your battalion," Yanosh said. "You have good company commanders."

I pushed a plate of food across the table to Yanosh and tried to lighten the atmosphere. "How would you like some 'jaundice'?"

"No, thanks," Yanosh smiled. "I prefer to be fit and well."

"Then maybe an iron ration?" I asked.

"Something to drink, if possible...."

Kako brought soft drinks and fruit, and Yanosh and I ate together. A short while later, he left for his temporary office in the camp while I went to my quarters to change into coveralls. Eitan, my deputy, came in.

"You're getting into coveralls?" he asked.

"Must set a personal example...."

"Okay, then I'll go and change, too."

Haggai, the operations officer, phoned me with instructions to prepare two tanks for the brigade commander's orders group—if we moved. I tried to appeal, arguing that it would break up my company formations. Haggai said that he understood, but objectively it was right to take them from me. I called Emmy, who had the largest company. He tried to persuade me not to give up two vehicles, but finally accepted the judgment.

"It seems to me that you should send Ami Doron and another tank commander, because they'll be working independently. I believe you'll manage without your deputy. It's more important that he should command the two tanks. Tell them that they'll rendezvous with the brigade commander at the crossroads and will move over to his radio frequency."

"Alright. But be ready for a visit from them. They'll appeal the decision."

"Okay. Only remember that a company commander must also know how to give unpleasant orders and to solve his own problems."

Emmy grasped that I was challenging him to settle the matter without further involving me.

The battalion continued to prepare rapidly. Gidi, the operations officer, and his sergeants took the maps off the walls. Each man packed his personal kit and lashed it to his tank. The headquarters group stowed theirs in their armored personnel carriers.

We received an order to evacuate the women personnel. Four had come up with the battalion. Naomi and Riki were in the battalion office, Shlomit in operations and Ophra on the armorer's staff. They had fit in well with life at Nafah. Naomi and Riki had gone on leave the day before. Shlomit and Ophra were helping with the packing and were not at all pleased that they were being evacuated. While the equipment was being taken out of the room, and in the presence of a few officers, Shlomit came over to me.

"Sir, what do you think? Will there be a war? Yes or no?"

I tried to stall.

"I don't think there will be a real war, but it's certainly possible that the Syrians will try to grab part of the Heights."

"What, for example?"

"The Rafid approaches, Tel Faress, and perhaps even Quneitra. It's important to them to show that they can succeed in doing something against us."

As we talked, those within hearing closed in on us. Yair Swet was listening intently, and Gidi and the operations sergeants stopped work.

"You're the only one in the battalion who took part in the Six-Day War," Shlomit persisted. "You have experience. How do you feel right now?"

"I feel good. The battalion is ready. The crews are well trained and that gives me confidence."

"Are you afraid?" she blurted out.

I had never been asked that question in such a personal way, in front of my subordinates, just as war was about to break out.

"Afraid? I don't know," I replied slowly. "That's not a question you can answer with a straight yes or no. You fear the unknown, but I know what we can expect and I don't need to be afraid. I haven't fought since I was wounded in the Six-Day War, and I don't know how I will react to be in a war again. Right now, none of us knows how it will develop. I would say that I am excited in a way about what will happen."

"After your Six-Day War experience," Shlomit went on, "I should imagine you would be more afraid."

"Yes, if the injury were to my spirit. But it was physical and so there's no reason. In any event, you should know that if the Syrians open fire, we will lay into them hard, real hard. We have a battalion of lions."

I hoped with that to change the tone of the conversation.

"Good luck," said Shlomit. She shook my hand, then joined Ophra as they headed for the transport that was waiting to evacuate them.

At 12:00, H-hour for completing preparations, the battalion was drawn up ready to move and to defend itself against air attack. All personal kits were lashed to tanks and armored personnel carriers. The crew were in their compartments. Every commander stood in his turret, a belt of 0.3 machine gun ammunition loaded and ready for firing. Camouflage nets were spread over the tanks. Battalion headquarters was assembled with vehicles across the road and ready to move. My tank and Eitan's stood by the office without nets. Gidi, who was to be fifth man in my crew, made a final check.

"Gidi, lash my parka to the tank. We might be cold tonight." He placed it next to the spare radio. It looked strange there on a hot day, but I wanted the men to feel that we were preparing for a major, and possibly long, operation.

The minutes passed by slowly. I called over my artillery support officer to refresh my memory on what was available. Avraham Snir, a lieutenant, came complete with coveralls, a gunbelt and maps.

"Snir, what can you give us when they open fire?"

"Sir, there will be a number of batteries at our disposal. But in any case, I have to request them from brigade artillery."

"You be prepared to give me fire where I need it without bothering me with angles and azimuths...."

"You only have to ask, and I'll give you what I can."

Artillery has always seemed to me to be something we can win without, perhaps because it doesn't do much harm to tanks.

"Are you set up in a tank?" I asked him.

"Yes, sir."

"I don't want you along just for the ride. Be prepared to operate the radio, load shells and use the machine gun."

"The crew has already taught me."

"Fine. Then return to your tank."

The radio nets were still closed. The time—almost 1300 hours. I ordered a relaxation of alert. I took a walk around the tanks so the men would see me, but not before ordering Kako to drive

behind me with an open radio. I didn't have much time. I had
to be with Yanosh at two. My first stop was at Zamir's company—"Tiger" on the radio net. Everything was in perfect order:
access pathways whitewashed, a parking space for a Jeep, taut
tents open for airing. Zamir saw me and came over.

"No wars, sir?"

"Wait. It's still quiet."

"Anything new?"

"Not yet. I'm going to brigade soon. Zamir, don't let the men
wander away from the tanks. You've got veterans from a company that's been operational, but if you allow the tension to
drop, you might find yourself ..."

"None of mine move without permission from me."

"How's morale?"

"They're used to alerts and to Golan, sir."

Captain Zamir was considered a good company officer, and
the state of his unit was evidence that he ran a tight ship and
could control his men. Amnon's company was standing by my
office. Since both my tank and Eitan's were part of Amnon's
force, I didn't go to them next but headed for Yair Swet's company, which was near the wadi north of the crossroads. There
were mattresses strewn on the ground by the tents—and it annoyed me. I called Yishai Zarhi, commander of Yair's Number
One Platoon.

"What are these mattresses doing here?"

"They arrived an hour ago, and we haven't had time to put
them away."

"Yishai, I don't want to see them. Get them into the tents
immediately!"

Yair came over in a hurry.

"I'll see to it, sir. We didn't have time...."

"Don't let tension break up routine. At moments like these
it's easy to loosen up, but you mustn't let it happen. How's the
company doing?"

"All the tanks are ready. We've got a traversing problem in
one of them, but the electrician is working on it."

Yair was tenser than usual.

"How do the boys feel? Nervous?"

"Some of them. It's understandable."

"Okay. Use the time to talk to your tank commanders and platoon officers—and use the map to explain."

Yair—"Vespa" on the radio net—was the veteran among the battalion's company commanders. He had run five consecutive courses for tank crewmen, and was fed up with it. He was due for release in February, so there wasn't much point to giving him a new job till then. He was already planning to join his father at Neviot, in Sinai, where Swet Senior—a World War II disabled veteran—was running a gasoline station. The old man was known in the neighborhood as "Ironside of Nuweiba"— the Arab name for Neviot—because of his wheelchair, the result of a double amputation. Yair talked of helping his parents with the gas station, and of guiding tours around Sinai. Meanwhile, he was very popular with his men, who were known to be ready to follow him—through fire and water.

My next call was on Menahem Albert's company, which I had moved away from battalion headquarters because the density would be extra dangerous in case of air attack. Now I saw tents next to a garbage pit that served the area, and that was a danger to the health of the men. Suddenly Amos Nahum, a second lieutenant and commander of Menahem's Number Three Platoon, ran across my path.

"Hey, Amos, what's happened?"

"The company commander has called in all the platoon officers. He wants to give us some instructions."

"He'll wait a moment. How's your platoon?"

"Ready to move," he said, obviously excited by the tension. I smiled.

"Okay. Go to the company commander. I'll be there soon."

Off he ran, field glasses jolting up and down on his chest, and helmet in hand.

Amos, a dedicated armor man, had come to us from Gash Battalion. During one of Yanosh's visits to us in Sinai, Amos— who had a highly developed sense of justice—had complained of discrimination against our battalion as regards equipment, allocation of furloughs and so on. I knew there was truth in what he said, but I was startled to find that he had gone as far as the brigade commander in making comparisons. The battalion had pulled together as a team and had a lot to be proud of, but

I couldn't help seeing the complaints as an attack on my leadership. Yanosh was no less offended at the suggestion of discrimination inside his brigade. I later found out that he had hauled his staff officers over the coals because of their neglect of our battalion. As for me, I expressed some of my pain and disappointment at the comparisons between battalions—and between men—at a dinner party for the battalion officers. My words were heard in heavy silence.

Albert's tanks were well camouflaged and altogether in too perfect an order. There was no way of knowing the difference between the vehicles of the platoon commanders and the others. The tactical markings on each tank were like the commander's signature, and I had learned to tell them apart by those markings.

Menahem Albert and his officers were bent over a map under one of the camouflage nets. By contrast, Emmy and his men were in a tent, sitting around a half-empty parcel someone had received from home. Between mouthfuls Emmy was issuing his orders, but he stopped as I sat down on one of the beds, and turned to me.

"Sir, H Company wants to know when we're moving up to our positions to screw the Syrians."

"You're talking as if I'm coordinating the Syrians."

"It's about time we taught them not to mess up our holidays."

"Emmy, we'll fight if we have to. I hope we won't have to."

The young officers studied me in surprise. Then Amir Bashari, one of Emmy's three veteran platoon sergeants, moved in on the conversation with his deep voice.

"We're fed up with shooting at barrels!"

"There's an advantage in barrels, Emmy. They can't shoot back at you."

"We're almost due for release, sir, and we haven't yet tasted fire."

"You've got a lot more years to live, and statistics say that there's a war every ten years, so don't worry about it."

"Sir," Emmy insisted, "What do you think? Is anything going to happen?"

"In my opinion—yes. I still don't know what. I'm going to brigade at two, and if there's anything new I'll let you know."

I walked back to my Jeep, very satisfied with what I had seen.

"Sir," Yoav Bluman, another of Emmy's triumvirate of sergeants, ran after me. "Can you spare me a moment?"

"Yes."

"I want to understand why I have to be the one to give my tank to the brigade commander."

"He'll sit in your tank—and you'll be the center of everything that's happening. It's an honor!"

"Look sir, I've trained hard and long for this only to give my tank to somebody else? There are so many young tank commanders ... "

"Yoav, your company has more tanks than any of the others, and the choice just happened to be you. I don't have time now, but if there are no new developments, I'll see what I can do for you."

I picked up my operations officer and intelligence officer, and Kako drove us up to Yanosh's office, only to find that the area was packed with vehicles.

"Gidi," I asked my operations officer, "have you brought all the maps?"

"Yes, apart from the one I left in your tank."

We were walking away from the Jeep when it happened—the whine of low-flying aircraft, then loud explosions that shook us and the buildings. I froze for a second, then looked up to see four MiGs dropping their bombs on the camp and on the men clustered around the vehicles. I felt helpless—didn't know which way to run. I fell to the ground by one of the buildings, pressed my head into the earth with my clasped palms above it. The explosions were coming nearer. I felt humiliated. Syrian planes were diving over an Israeli camp, doing whatever they wanted. Raising my head to look around, my eyes met those of Ratess and a familiar face made me feel a little better.

"To your tanks!"

Yanosh was shouting as he ran towards his APC. I scrambled back into my Jeep, this time in the driver's seat, as my two officers hauled themselves onto the rear bench and Kako slid into place next to me. The road to the camp gate was packed with vehicles on their way out. For a moment, I thought of running the two thousand yards to Nafah, then I swung the Jeep over the fence, ripping out barbed wire as I climbed up onto the main road, and gunned the motor.

12

OCTOBER 6, 1973—
DAY OF ATONEMENT AFTERNOON

"Where's the microphone?" I yelled at the two men crouched on the back seat between maps, battle rations and items of equipment. The battalion intelligence officer, probably quite appropriately, was the one who found it.

"All 'policemen' stations, this is the battalion commander! Start engines! Prepare to move! Over and out."

I shoved hard down on the accelerator, but the Jeep still seemed to crawl. We would make a good target, alone on the road, if the planes came back.

"All 'policemen,' " I repeated into the mike, "This is the battalion commander. Secure nets and stand by to move. Over."

"Emmy reporting. All okay. We'll be ready in a few minutes. Over."

"Amnon here. Ready to move immediately. Over."

"Menahem reporting. Ready immediately. Over."

"Zamir here. Ready. Over."

"Yair here. Ready. Over."

"Eitan here. Ready. Your tank is waiting with me. Over."

" 'Policeman' here. I'm on my way to the tank. Deploy immediately. Over."

There were no planes in the sky, but shells were beginning to fall around the quarry at the crossroads. My tank was standing, its engine running, at the roadside. Kilyon, the gunner, was in the turret, holding the machine gun, waiting for me to replace him. I stopped the Jeep alongside and leaped straight up to the turret. Gidi, the operations officer, followed me in and took his place on the radioman/loader's seat. We locked into the intercom net—and I suddenly felt a wave of relief. My fear of not reaching the tank from which I would command the battalion was over.

"All 'police' stations, this is the CO. I want a wide spread, so vehicles won't be hit. Report situation. Over."

"Yair reporting. Ready to move, but I'm unable to deploy in my area. Have to cross the road. Over."

Menahem and Amnon reported that they were in place. Ami and Zamir said their areas were too tight, and asked permission to move. Granted.

"Yanosh stations—this is Yanosh."

The battalion commanders reported one by one.

"Haim here. On my way to the vehicles. Over."

"Kahalani here. In place at the crossroads. Deployed and ready to move."

"Ratess here. On my way to vehicles."

"Yos here. Moving to my place."

"Yanosh here. Speed it up! Out."

Yanosh's two APCs moved along the road from Nafah crossing to Quneitra. The crossroads was under constant artillery fire, but—for all that I was scared they would be hit, and impressed by their courage—the two vehicles got through and raced on up the road. There was a strange dryness in my mouth. The tanks were rolling across the terrain, and I was waiting for orders. On the brigade radio, Ben-Shoham was asking Yanosh for a battalion, according to the commanding general's instructions. I could guess that it wasn't an easy decision. Finally Yanosh ordered Haim, who was at Sindiana, to transfer to Ben-Shoham's command. The sector was split into two, with Ben-Shoham taking southern Golan and Yanosh the center and north.

"Crew, what did you do when the planes came?" I asked over the intercom.

"Kilyon fired at them," Gideon the loader offered.

"A belt and a half of ammo," Kilyon summed up.

"And how many did you hit?" I asked.

He took me seriously. The reply was distinctly apologetic.

"They were bombing the camp—not us. It was too far."

"How many were there?"

"Six to eight."

I clipped my map onto a board that I had fixed outside the cupola, then cleared away some empty cartridge cases that were lying on the turret.

"Kahalani—this is the brigade commander. Come in. Over."

"Kahalani here."

"Send a company to Waset Junction to report to Yos."

So I was to lose a company, too.

"Yanosh here. Your location? Over."

"Still deployed at the crossroads. Waiting for orders."

"Stay there, ready to move."

Who was I going to send? I knew none of the company commanders wanted to leave the battalion. I decided to send Emmy—the closest to the road.

"Emmy, battalion commander here. Over."

"Emmy here. Over."

"You still have the two tanks you were to give to the brigade commander?"

"I have them. I hope he's forgotten them."

"Maybe there's no need for them. From now on you're under Yos' command. He's at Waset Junction. Switch to his frequency and establish contact."

"When do I return to battalion?"

"I don't know. Now move out."

He ordered his company to converge and began to move.

"Emmy here. The track near the road isn't good. It'll slow me down."

"Battalion commander here. Step on the gas."

"Okay, but I want permission to use the road."

I remembered Ben-Shoham and the commanding general insisting that the narrow roads of Golan must be preserved at all cost. I didn't want Emmy delayed, but on the other hand didn't feel like explaining why I had allowed a company to use the road—if it turned out to be a minor incident.

"Emmy, I'll leave it to your judgment."

"Emmy here. Okay, be seeing you."

He used the road.

We waited another hour at the crossroads, still expecting orders. I didn't want to waste fuel so I ordered the engines silenced.

"Brigade commander to Kahalani."

"Receiving. Over."

"Start moving east. Over."

"Where to? Over."

"Towards the ridges south of Quneitra."

"Affirmed. Out."

Zamir and his company were on the east axis, close to the road, so I ordered him to lead the battalion. The tanks rolled on a dirt track near the road, raising clouds of dust. It was slow going, so I decided to move onto the paved road. We still couldn't see the border and hadn't encountered enemy fire. The sun was at our backs. There were occasional explosions of shells, and distant smoke columns rising to the sky. Apart from the deep track marks gouged in the asphalt, it could have been an Independence Day parade. We were rolling fast, at fixed distances, guns pointing alternately left and right, commanders upright in the turrets of smartly turned-out tanks. Of course, the turret panniers packed high with gear might have raised eyebrows in the reviewing stands, but otherwise....

From the exchanges on the radio I understood that Yos was heading for the border and Ratess was in the area of the Hermonit.

"Yanosh to Kahalani. Over."

"Kahalani here. Go ahead. Over."

"Change of mission. Move to take position on the ridges north of Quneitra facing east. A large Syrian task force is approaching the town."

"Affirm. Over."

I was already thinking about our route to Quneitra.

"I want one tank company, under your deputy, to move on the ridge where you were heading."

"Affirmed. Over."

"Your deputy will switch to my frequency. From now on, he's an independent brigade force."

"Okay. Right now I'm on the road between Shifon and Yossefun. You want me to go round Bental and Avital from the west till I reach the road north of them?" I asked, referring to the two extinct volcanoes that towered over the landscape.

"Why? Over."

"That way I'll come straight into position."

"No. I want you to take the shortest route."

Zamir was nearest to the ridges, so I transferred him under the command of Eitan, to the brigade. Zamir didn't ask many questions, and Eitan sounded satisfied at having an independent unit.

Then I turned the battalion, less two companies, on to dirt tracks that led to Kibbutz Ein Zivan. My tank led the battalion. The kibbutz was deserted, and its access road and fields were pitted with shell craters. I don't like taking tanks through towns. They're vulnerable to snipers and bazooka teams, and besides, only one tank can really fight at a time. If the lead tank is crippled, the whole column stops. So I decided not to go through Quneitra, but across the fields of Kibbutz Meron Golan—after warning the tank commanders to be careful not to damage irrigation pipes.

We deployed on the 5-foot-high earthen ramps on top of Booster Ridge, with Menahem facing east to Quneitra, Yair facing northeast, and Amnon and I looking directly due east. The tanks were close together, and the ramps weren't really designed to allow us to fire from under their shelter. The sun was sinking, but we could clearly see pillars of dust to the east, moving towards us. One of our forward positions was located on the Quneitra-Damascus road. It was supported by six tanks from Ben-Shoham's force under the command of Lieutenant Colonel Yair, who was reporting constant Syrian movement towards the frontier.

13

OCTOBER 6, 1973—
DAY OF ATONEMENT   EVENING

A hail of artillery fire struck our positions. They had found us. The blast was heavy enough to be felt inside the tanks, and splinters of black basalt rock were hailing down on us together with the shrapnel. I ordered the company commanders to tell their men to duck inside their turrets.

"Battalion commander, this is 'Zilia,' " someone called over the radio.

"Repeat. Over."

I couldn't understand who would use that code name right now. Maybe Menahem making a mistake—but it wasn't his voice.

"I repeat, this is 'Zilia' calling battalion commander."

"The real 'Zilia'?"

"Affirmative."

"You're nuts! What are you doing here?"

"I came to fight. I want to join you. Where are you?"

"On Booster Ridge. There's a war here. Hold on."

"Okay. I'm looking for a tank."

"Zilia" was Efraim Laor, who, up to three months before, had been commander of G Company, then got himself thrown in prison for driving a Jeep without a license; the Jeep overturned and all his passengers were injured. Laor's men liked him and he was a good officer. I asked Yanosh to post him back to battalion after his prison sentence, but the brigade commander said that because of the offense, he couldn't return as a company commander. None of that mattered now. Laor was back.

As darkness fell, we stood helpless under accurate Syrian artillery fire. I ordered the tanks to spread out, then heard over the radio that Yos, with Emmy's company, had made contact with Syrian tanks. Yos, who was in an APC south of the Hermonit Tel, was asking for flares. Soon the darkening sky was lit by eerie, unnatural light as Yos' tanks picked off an occasional enemy target.

Yair, the colonel down by our forward position, reported that Syrian tanks were moving in on Quneitra from the south of Booster Ridge. Yanosh asked if I could see them.

"Negative."

"Kahalani, this is Yanosh. Make sure that some of your vehicles are overlooking the town and ready to block in that direction."

"From where I am we can't block the entrance. It's too dark."

"Maybe you can move a few tanks forward...."

"Negative. Better to send a company to the east of the town, and let them block there."

"Okay. Make sure they deploy well, and report any contact with enemy."

I ordered Menahem to take his company into the town and to deploy near the Military Police Station. He knew the area but didn't know how to get there from Bustar, so I directed him down as far as the road. He moved into the town, from where we could hear explosions and see flames.

Syrian tanks were closing in on Yos, so I ordered Yair to move out beyond the ramp that blocked his fire, and to take a position facing northeast, with his tanks in line abreast so they could all fire without obstruction. Because of the difficulty of moving in the dark, it was some minutes before Yair requested permission to open fire.

"Okay. The fire must be rapid, at the discretion of each tank commander. Remember this is a war."

I stood between Yair's tanks, trying to identify the enemy. From the occasional flares, it was obvious that we couldn't hit them. Yos began to complain that he wasn't getting illumination, and tried hard to keep his temper when Arye, the brigade artillery officer, replied that he was short of flare shells but would have more in a half an hour. Meanwhile Yanosh asked me to supply gunfire in support of Yos.

"I'll try, but the range is too great."

The Syrian tank drivers were using infrared headlamps to avoid detection with the naked eye, so I studied the terrain with an infrared detector scope that permits us to see at night. There were headlamps—a long way off. Yos was still reporting contact with enemy tanks. Ratess had deployed his force over a wide area north of Hermonit, a 750-foot-high Tel. Eitan and Zamir were south of Quneitra. There were big gaps between our front-line positions, and we had to deploy to cover all the terrain. I wasn't happy with my present position. To the east were Yair's tanks from Ben-Shoham's force, and I couldn't use my guns in that direction. I thought of joining Yos, who was under attack, but that would have meant leaving positions that controlled the terrain—and moving away from Menahem's company in Quneitra. I was troubled by the feeling that we were doing nothing, and somewhere deep inside was the thought that I was going to miss the war. Nobody could know what was going to happen.

"Kahalani to brigade commander. Over."

"Yanosh here. Over."

"Up on this ridge I'm ineffective. I'm firing at the tanks moving towards Yos, but it's a waste of ammunition. Since some of Ben-Shoham's crews are east of me, I suggest joining Yos."

"I don't want to lose control over Booster."

"I've thought of that. I have a reduced unit commanded by Amnon. I'll leave them here."

"Okay. Coordinate with Yos and move out to his positions."

I ordered Yair to follow me westward on the road down from Bustar. He confirmed but needed time to collect his company. Shells were still falling on our positions as I waited on the road for Yair and his tanks.

"Yair, what's happening? Over."

"I'll be there in a minute. Two of my tanks are having trouble with rocks, and I think one has dropped a track."

I could feel the tension mount. It wasn't going to be easy getting a tank out of there at night—under shellfire.

"Are you sure?"

"Hold on. I'm going down to see for myself."

"Right. Be quick."

I brought my tank up close enough to see one of Yair's tanks standing askew in a pit. Yair was there trying to guide the commander of the stuck vehicle. Time was pressing. Yos needed help.

Yair was back on the radio, puffing from the exertion.

"One of my tanks is in a pit—and has dropped its track."

"What about the other?"

"Okay and ready to move."

"Alright. Attach a tow to another tank and pull that one under the ramp, then follow me."

At first I really thought of leaving it, but it stood on the forward slope and would be helpless in daylight.

"Do I leave another tank for assistance?"

"No. Amnon's staying. He'll look after it later. Amnon, are you listening?"

"Amnon here. Affirmative."

The tank was finally in a safe place. With Yair's tanks behind me on the road, we started to move. Yuval, my driver, switched on his infrareds and started to move fast. I ordered him to shut them off in case the Syrians could detect us.

"I can't see a thing."

"I'll guide you."

I picked up the mike of the battalion net radio.

"This is the battalion commander. Don't use your infrared lights. We can drive by moonlight."

Gidi directed Yuval, who couldn't see a thing and went off the road a few times. Our drivers were trained to drive on roads where the steering was much finer. But the clatter of the tanks behind us gave a feeling of power. My eyes were on the road ahead all the time, not that I could see much. We had reached the Quneitra-Mas'ade road and turned towards Tel Bar-On crossroads when phosphor shells began to descend. It was a regular fireworks display. I told Yair to pick up speed through the crossroads. It was zeroed in.

"Yos to brigade commander. Over."

His voice sounded strange.

"Brigade commander here. Go ahead. Over."

"I'm wounded. Am evacuating to rear."

"What happened?"

Yanosh was worried.

"Shrapnel. It's okay. I can make it alone."

"Alright."

Yos was hit close to his eyes. Later, as he was being evacuated in an APC, it crashed into one of the tanks and he was injured in the shoulder. Yos dressed his own wounds, then moved out to the rear. Meanwhile, I realized that I was now responsible for his sector. I switched to the frequency of Emmy's company and told him that he was returning from Yos' command to battalion command. I knew the terrain from a reconnaissance we had made a week before. The road through the positions was known as "Tarzan," and the name had stuck in my memory. Emmy was happy to be back. He filled me in on the situation.

"We hit a number of tanks that tried to ascend the positions."

"All okay with you?"

"Seems so. I haven't yet had reports from all the tanks. But I think B1 has gone."

"Who?"

"B1. My deputy, Doron, has gone to see. As soon as I have details I'll let you know."

Amir Bashari, I thought to myself. I knew the code numbers of all the tank commanders in the company.

Kilyon was just telling Gideon, "You hear that? Bashari's dead," when Emmy was back.

"Battalion commander, this is Emmy."

"Go ahead, over."

"It's confirmed. B1 has had it. The crew is okay and the tank seems alright."

"Where is it?"

"The driver took it to the rear."

"I don't understand. Where's the crew?"

"The turret crew is with my deputy, and the driver is moving to the crossroads."

"Alone? How does he know where he's going?"

"You're right. It wasn't under my control. I'll try to make contact with him and I'll report back."

The details came out later. Amir's tank had been firing into the valley where the Syrians were advancing. Moshe Uliel, his gunner, hit perhaps ten of them, and most caught fire. At 21:30 they took a hard blow, and Amir fell inside. A shell had hit the command cupola, killing him instantly. Uliel and Ganani, the loader/radioman, jumped out to take cover between the rocks, waiting for someone to tell them what to do. Ami Doron, Em-

my's deputy, arrived and ordered the driver to evacuate Amir.
The tank turned west without any guide or crew and vanished
into the night. Uliel and Ganani came out of the rocks and
jumped on a tank to tell Emmy what had happened. Doron later
collected them and told them to sit in the turret panniers till
they could be evacuated.

After the war, I found out that the driver had headed west as
ordered, but realizing that he couldn't find the road in the dark,
he jumped out—leaving Amir's body inside. He ran westward,
passing our forces who took him for a Syrian and opened fire.
He was wounded in the legs and packed off to the hospital.
Right through the war, and for a week after it, we had him listed
as missing.

Amir Bashari. Our first battalion casualty. How many hours
was it since he asked when we were going to stop shooting at
barrels?

14

OCTOBER 6, 1973   NIGHT

I arrived at the new positions and divided the sector into two: Emmy would take the side closest to the Hermonit, and Yair the area down to the road to the south of us. Our tanks spread out in the dark. Occasional shells fell in the area, but they didn't particularly bother us. In the darkness, I couldn't tell how the tanks were deployed and was uncertain that the enemy couldn't penetrate. There was a silhouette of a rise that seemed to control the terrain. I moved slowly towards it, checking on a map. It was Tel Jit, close to the road leading to our easternmost position. The crew were tense, and the gloom around us prevented any initiative on our part. I asked for a couple of mortar shells on the valley below, then strained my eyes to spot enemy tanks— but it was useless. One of my tanks fired and I could see a flash where the shell hit, then a Syrian tank that had tried to get up to us. He wasn't hit, and we were short of star shells. But we went on trying to spot them by moonlight.

"Snir, this is the battalion commander," I called my artillery officer.

"Snir here. Over."

"My friend, I ask nothing else of you—just light up the area."

"Sir, I'm asking all the time from higher up."

"Yell at them. I want illumination!"

I was trying hard to sound angry.

"Right."

"Yair and Emmy, this is the battalion commander. I don't know when we'll get flares. You must keep your eyes peeled. Use your scopes to spot them as they come."

"Battalion commander, this is Emmy. There are fifteen of them coming towards me. I'm waiting for them."

"Hold on," I said while I scanned the area with my infrascope. Their infrared lights were stronger than their headlamps. Without the scope, I couldn't see a thing. With it, I could pick out pairs of lamps.

"Okay, Emmy. I see them. As soon as you can hit, start firing."

"They don't know what's waiting for them. Over."

"Don't crow! We both know you can't target them."

Our tanks were fitted with peri-telescopes that worked beautifully by day or on illuminated targets at night, but couldn't pick up infrared lights. There was no doubt, I thought, that the T-55s were more advanced than our tanks, especially when it came to night firing. We knew it from the Six-Day War, but little attention had been paid to the fact. The Syrian movement towards us by night was worrying. I had learned that armored warfare at night was usually our prerogative. I knew that we were working with a terrible limitation, and that they could do their target finding with infrared searchlights—without us even knowing it.

"Battalion commander to Snir. What's the situation? Over."

"I'm doing the maximum."

"Brigade commander, this is Kahalani."

I had decided to pass the problem on to Yanosh.

"Yanosh here. Go ahead."

"Enemy tanks facing and moving towards us. Can't estimate number. They're using I.a. [infrared] and I don't have to tell you our limitations. I must have illumination."

"There are no shells at the moment. I hope there will be within half an hour. Meanwhile use your searchlights."

"Kahalani here. I have searchlights, but I prefer not to use them."

"I know the problems, but there is no other way at the moment."

Searchlights, I told myself, were certain death. The Syrians were 300 yards away. Light beams would attract fire on the tank that was doing the job. I didn't order their use—but left it up to individual tank commanders. The moon was now full, and indistinct dust columns could be seen in the distance.

"David," I called my gunner.

"Sir, call me Kilyon."

"About time you changed your name. Okay, David, I want you to try to find Syrians by moonlight."

"I can't see anything."

"But a strong will can overcome anything. . . ."

I swung the gun in the direction from which I expected the Syrians to come. Near my firing position, beyond the ruins of some houses damaged in the previous war, were clumps of foliage that were swaying in the light wind. I imagined that I saw figures slipping through the bushes. Again I scanned the area through my scope—and picked up a pair of infrared lights coming directly at me. I adjusted the gun setting somewhat crudely and ordered Kilyon to be ready with a HEAT shell.

"Direction?" he asked.

"It's okay, I'll show you."

We fired one, more to scare the enemy than anything else. I couldn't see where it hit. I took another look through the scope. The headlamps were still approaching. Then I suddenly realized that my tank was completely illuminated. When I put down the scope we were in the dark again. We had been caught dead center in the beam of an infrared projector. The Syrian was targetting in on us.

"Driver! Back up! Quickly! Move!" I screamed.

Yuval slipped his gears into reverse—but it was slow.

"Move!"

The engine roared with full power, and the tank rocked back over slabs of stone and terrace walls till we came to a stop at the bottom of the hill.

"We were being set up. A tank had his projector on us," I explained.

"How do you know?" Gidi asked.

"I could see that we were lit up when I used my infrascope to look for his. We had more luck than sense."

I guided the tank into a new position, then noticed a red lamp burning among the silhouettes of my tanks.

"All 'policeman' stations, this is the battalion commander. Check that all lights are doused!"

A few minutes passed but the light was still there.

"Yair and Emmy, there's a rear or brake light burning on one of your tanks. Douse it immediately."

They both reported that all lights were out. I was getting angry.

"Battalion commander here. I want you to check tank by tank. Over."

Again they reported that all lights were out. I took a look at the offender through field glasses, and could vaguely see exhaust fumes. Thinking for a moment that one of the drivers might not be familiar with all his panel switches, I ordered all engines switched off.

"Ami and Emmy, the tank that I'm talking about—its engine is still running."

"I personally vouch that all my engines are shut down," reported Emmy.

"This is Yair. The light's in my area, but all my tanks have reported shutting down."

I remembered an incident with a strange tank during the Six-Day War—it turned out to be a maverick from another battalion. Better be careful! We could turn a searchlight on it, but that would endanger the operator.

"Yair, this is the battalion commander. I want your tank to be ready to light up the suspect tank."

There was no answer. If the tank was a Syrian, it could be targetting us with infrared without us even knowing. While waiting for Yair to respond, I shouted into the crew intercom.

"Gunner, prepare to fire."

"Which direction? I can't see a thing."

"Hold it. I'll tell you."

I switched to the external net.

"Yair, this is the battalion commander. Did you receive my last message?"

"Yair here. A moment and I'll tell you which vehicle is ready to fire."

"Negative. I want your tank to give me illumination. I'll fire."

"Alright. One moment."

"Sir, loader here, shell in breech."

"Good. Gunner, you ready?"

"Yes, sir. What range?"

"Doesn't matter much. Make it 100 yards."

"Battalion commander, sir, this is Yair's number three, ready
to provide beam."

Number three. That would be Boaz Eliav, the stout boy from
Jerusalem. Father a retired colonel. I'd given him a month's
special leave so he could diet. But for the war, he would have
been home in the Old City now.

"Battalion commander here. Your projector in good shape?"

"Affirmative."

"Your location?"

"Near the suspect."

"Flick a torch in my direction."

Much as I tried, I couldn't see him.

"Fire a machine-gun burst upwards ... Okay. I've got you.
Now listen. I'm ready to fire. Point your projector roughly at
him and wait till I tell you to turn it on."

"Right, sir."

This was going to be one hell of a joke if it was a tank of ours.

"Sir, Boaz here. Ready."

"Fine, now hold it."

I switched to the intercom.

"Kilyon, you ready?"

"Yes, sir, but I can't see anything."

"Don't fire till I tell you. It might be one of ours. Gideon, have
you released the safety?"

"Yes, sir."

Gidi was crouched back out of the way of the gun's recoil,
holding a fresh shell ready to reload.

"Boaz."

"Sir."

"Switch on."

I was hoping Boaz wouldn't be hit. Gripping my glasses, I
looked down Boaz' beam straight at a Syrian T-55—50 yards
from me.

"Fire!"

With a boom the shell was gone, its flash dazzling my eyes.
I strained to see if we had hit. Boaz switched off the beam. A
flame climbed slowly by the suspect. A horrible thought that
maybe I had been wrong was dispelled as I saw the flash elim-
inator on his gun. Only T-55s had those.

"Sir, Yair here, there's a suspect tank next to me," his voice broke the moment of radio silence.

"I don't see him. Check that it's enemy and destroy immediately."

A second Syrian tank stood within the arc of illumination of the burning tank. Since it hadn't moved so far, I didn't notice. But now they seemed to have realized their predicament. I bent down and swung the gun traverse towards the moving enemy.

"Gunner, be ready to fire."

"Ready. I see him," Kilyon sounded excited.

A sudden flash from a tank next to mine, and the intruder burst into flames.

"Nice. Who fired?"

"Yair here. It was Yishai, sir."

Yishai Zarhi. Commander of Number One Platoon in Yair's company. A slow-moving farmer from Nahalal, but put him in command of a platoon and you had a different man: fast, decisive, aggressive.

The two Syrians were blazing like torches against the night sky. Poor guys. They didn't know where they were. A soldier covered in flames ran like crazy from one of the tanks into the rocks and started to roll on the ground in a desperate attempt to kill the fire. Everything fogged over as pictures from seven years past flickered by my eyes.

15

JUNE 6, 1967

On the first day of the Six-Day War, I was rolling towards el-Arish, in northern Sinai. My battalion commander and Gonen, the brigade commander, were riding with my company. A victor's grin was on my lips as the Patton chewed up the black tarmac road between eucalyptus trees. It was about five in the evening, and I had visions of being the first to reach el-Arish. I was going to make history.

Suddenly a soldier jumped out into the road. I was about to fire when I saw he was one of ours. "Watch it! There are tanks!" he screamed.

Wondering how somebody could have got here before me, I slowed the tank and swung onto the nearby ridge. My tank was a mass of holes and dents from enemy fire. The gun mechanism had stopped functioning after a crash with a UN truck at Rafah. Only the machine guns and the engine were functioning. It was my third tank since morning. We stopped and I surveyed the landscape: foliage-covered ridges and trenches along the road. The sun was in the west, and shining in my eyes. I saw no tanks. Alon, who had been following, swung in beside me to serve as my gun. I directed him to traverse the turret towards the darkened ridges, then bent down to tell Rafi, my gunner, that he should try to spot the enemy through his sights. Suddenly the tank bucked and I felt a flame sear my back.

"Jump, we've been hit!" I yelled, not quite understanding what was happening.

The flame was cutting into my back like a knife. I tried to get away from it, and fell into the turret. I wanted to scream. Straining my legs and arms, I tried to push up through the cupola—but didn't have the strength. The smell of burning and a wave of intense heat swept the tank. I had to get out. I tried again, but fell back. I had a drowning man's vision—a last view of faces: my father, mother, my sister Ilana, Emanuel, Arnon, friends, home, Dalia.

"What's happening to me?" I screamed. "I'm coming apart!"

Closing my eyes I made a supreme effort to lift myself the three feet to the opening above me. I made it. Standing on the commander's seat, I tipped my torso out and rolled onto the engine cowling. I couldn't stand it anymore.

"Mother, I'm burning. I'm burning! I'm burning!"

I jumped down. Our tanks were racing around in panic. We were in an ambush—and I felt alone. . . . The others had problems of their own, and nobody had time for me. Me! The company commander, who had led them this far, who self-confidently had issued crisp orders, who exemplified courage in battle—I was in flames, running around alone, far from my burning tank. As I ran, the wind whipped up the flames. Throwing myself on the ground, I rolled in the dunes, ending up on my back. I scooped up sand with my burnt hands to cover my legs and belly. Ah, that eased the pain, and I wanted to sleep. But the tanks rolling by on both sides sent me shooting to my feet; I shook off the sand and ran from artillery shells that were exploding all around. Everything was burnt except my boots, a few tattered remnants of my blouse and a strip of underpants hanging from my body.

A Patton was coming up, not yet in the firing area. I ran to it and somehow hauled myself into the loader's compartment. It was Ilan Maoz' tank.

"Ilan, get me out of here," I yelled.

"Okay, Kahalani, don't worry."

The shaken loader helped me pull off the scraps of cloth from a body that felt like burning coals. My left sock had caught fire inside my boot, and they helped me take it off. Pulling back, Ilan helped me out of the tank onto a reconnaissance Jeep—naked as the day I was born. The Jeep passed the brigade commander's half-track. He and his staff officers stared in silence.

Maybe I had been saved, I told myself, but what of my men? I felt that I had let them down. How could I have let the enemy hit me like that?

16

The fiery Syrian vanished into the dark and the two wounded tanks blew up.

"All 'policeman' stations, this is the battalion commander. Check that there are no more Syrians in the area and warn all your crews."

Menahem occasionally reported from his positions among the ruined houses of Quneitra.

"Battalion commander, Menahem here. We're under constant heavy artillery fire."

"Can you identify any of their tanks? That worries me more than the artillery."

"I think so—but they're still out of range."

"Menahem, remember you are in a built-up area. Make sure your machine guns are trained on the points where infantry can approach!"

Our engines were still shut down so we could hear approaching Syrians. They have a distinctive, loud noise, completely unlike our relatively muffled tanks.

"Sir, Emmy here. I see a group. It's hard to judge the distance, but I estimate they're near the anti-tank ditch."

"Hold on."

I scanned the area with my glasses, spotted them, then ducked into the turret to take a look at the map.

"Emmy, I make it about 2,000 yards. Snir, you've got to illuminate the area. They seem to be crossing there, and I want artillery on them."

"Snir here. I'll try."

He indeed managed to get a few flare shells, then gave an azimuth and range, and to my surprise, shells began to fall among the Syrians. This officer was talented, I had to admit, and his artillery was not disappointing.

From Emmy's area, there was the sudden noise of Centurions. I asked him why he was moving tanks. He answered that he was deploying better. He was the only one among us who had seen the terrain in daylight, and he now suggested that we all move forward 100 yards.

"Battalion commander, Emmy here. Two of my tanks are in holes. They need a tow."

That was all I needed right now.

"Where are they?"

"To my left, on a low tel near Hermonit."

"Can you see them?"

"Negative. They're too far."

I couldn't pinpoint the place.

"Battalion commander, there are enemy vehicles moving west, to the north of me."

I could see four infrared headlamps.

"Emmy, I have them, but is that the direction of your stuck tanks?"

"Affirmative. It's difficult to tell, but the two Syrians seem to be passing between me and my Number Two Platoon."

Hell, they could get the two snagged tanks.

"Emmy, keep your engines off. Prepare to fire, and tell the crews of the two stuck vehicles to be in their places ready to fire if the Syrians approach them."

"Confirmed."

The Syrians were heading towards Kibbutz El-Rom and hadn't noticed us. I ordered Emmy to leave them alone. Either they were confused—or they were the vanguard of forces in the valley below.

Emmy sent Doron to extricate his two lame ducks. Doron groped through the dark, careful not to encounter the two Syrian marauders, found Avi and Barzilai and towed them clear. An hour later, the two Syrians headed back towards the clump of armor at the anti-tank ditch. They seemed to have lost their unit—a frequent occurence among armor.

Meanwhile, about six miles behind us at Waset Junction, Dr. Alex and his half-track, the communications officer and his command car, and the armorer officer with his APC had been circling around trying to find shelter from the constant shellfire. Dr. Alex finally unpacked his boxes and set up a casualty receiving station. The armorer was out of work. Technical repairs would mean coming forward to the tanks—and that wasn't possible. Kobi, the communications officer, was fuming that his vehicle offered no protection against artillery.

Dr. Alex received his first patient—a loader/radioman from Yair's company whose finger had been smashed by an 0.3 bullet from the tank's own machine gun. The medical team descended on him, ready to give their best to this, their first casualty of the war. Then a discussion started: which form had to be filled in? Was it the customary "injury on exercises" or was it "combat casualty"? He was evacuated to the rear without any paperwork.

Two hours later, the first tank reached the rear evacuation point. First Sergeant Bluman's tank had been hit by a Syrian. Bluman, unable to find the point of damage, had been given permission to pull back. The Syrian shell had hit the hull at the point where turret and housing met, putting the turret traverse out of commission. All the battalion fitters descended on their customer, eager for news of the war. The armorer officer found serious damage made by an armor-piercing shell. Lucky to be alive, Bluman and his crew headed for a collection point. They would be back two days later with a new tank.

Down on the approaches to Quneitra, where "Zechar" Company was under heavy bombardment, Menahem Albert strained to see signs of a Syrian advance. Suddenly he collapsed inside the turret, blood flowing from a gash on his forehead. Reuven Halfi, his loader/radioman, dressed the wound. Menahem was mumbling, "I want to reach Damascus."

The crew barely understood what he was saying. But one thing was clear. He refused to be evacuated—or parted from his field glasses. Holding them to his eyes, he insisted that he could carry on. Ronnie, the gunner, held his head, while Reuven reported to Avinoam that the company commander was injured. Menahem was transferred to an evacuation half-track together with Reuven, who had a shrapnel splinter in his back. Eitan Zeiman, commander of Number One Platoon, took over the company. Menahem's deputy overturned his tank trying to back clear of the bombardment area. The tank was upside down in a pit, but the turret cupola was open enough to let the crew crawl out. Ami Fargo, the deputy company commander, had smashed hands.

Hearing the dismal situation report from "Zechar" Company, I decided that I would rather have Eitan, my deputy, in command down there. He switched into the company net and began to give orders for the continued block on the town. I had a few moments of anxiety over confused reports of events in Quneitra. First I was told that the town was under attack by tanks, but it turned out to be artillery. Menahem's injury and the company's distance from me gave me a feeling that the company was abandoned—but Eitan was there, I reassured myself.

I was tired. War or no war, I was dropping off. I washed my eyes, but it only helped for a few minutes. It was already very late. The moon was sinking, and a frightening silence blanketed the area. Syrian tank lights blinked in the distance—how far away I could not tell. I thought of how fortunate Joshua was: "Sun, stand still upon Gibeon, and moon in the Valley of Ayalon." How I yearned for the sun to rise!

"Snir, we're about to get total darkness. No moon. Scream, threaten—I don't care what you do—we must have star shells."

"Snir here. I have just been allocated a battery. They're on their way to you. You want me to illuminate the crossing at the anti-tank ditch?"

"Negative. The crossing doesn't worry me right now. Be ready to illuminate the area in front of our positions."

"Okay."

They must all be tired like me. I fixed night schedules. The drivers could sleep, on condition that they could be awakened instantly. The rest could take turns, but two men must be awake at all times, their bodies half out of the turrets. Even as I dozed, questions flitted through my tired brain: What was happening in southern Golan? What was happening at home? My father and brother Emanuel had probably been mobilized. What did the people at home know about us?

Amnon, with four tanks, was in the Booster area, in control from a height. He reported movement a long way off. He started to fire at the Syrians, but I told him not to waste ammunition.

17

OCTOBER 7, 1973   MORNING

Four in the morning. First light. Gidi and I took turns commanding the tank while Kilyon and Gideon slept in rotation. I tried to sleep, but the radio calls kept rousing me.

The two blackened Syrian hulks stood 50 yards away. The atmosphere was tense. What would happen at dawn? Would they continue their offensive? Would we find that Syrian tanks had passed us by?

"All 'policeman' stations. Battalion commander here."

I checked that all the company commanders were awake.

"Start engines and activate all systems. Be ready for battle at dawn. Everyone is to be awake and in position ready for movement."

The thunder of engines and the black smoke of exhausts filled the air. I was reminded of the roar of lions—ready to pounce on their prey. To the north, the bulk of Hermonit loomed high above us in the morning light. To the south, I could see Booster Ridge. We were in a valley about 100 yards from the earthen ramps that had been prepared as tank positions, and I now ordered the battalion to move forward onto the ramps.

"Battalion commander. This is Emmy. Do you want me to bring my two tanks down from the foot of Hermonit?"

"If they're in good positions—negative."

"Very good. I'm leaving the platoon up there."

Sergeant Yisrael Barzilai, whose tank was close to the Hermonit, moved into a firing position, drew out a camera and photographed the tanks that were charging us, then—and only then—aimed his gun and fired a shell at the enemy wave.

" 'Policeman' stations. Move up to your positions slowly. There are Syrians behind the ramp."

The vehicles rolled forward, leaving behind them billowing clouds of black dust. I brought up the rear so I could check on the deployment. The first tanks moved into position, their commanders upright in the turrets. Suddenly a shell was fired from somewhere in Emmy's company line, and a cloud of dust rose around the tank that fired. Before the dust settled, another shell was on its way.

"This is the battalion commander. Who fired?"

No answer. I couldn't see what he was firing at. The company commanders weren't responding, and I could only assume that they were checking on their command radios. I waited.

"Emmy here. One of mine moved up, identified a stranger at close quarters and fired."

Could a tank have been there all night? It must be one that was damaged, and Emmy's Number One Platoon commander had fired without checking.

"Battalion commander, Yair here."

He was excited.

"Go ahead, Yair."

"Number of enemy tanks in my sector, moving towards us. Am taking position and opening fire."

"Driver, take us forward fast. Kilyon, prepare to fire. Gidi, check that the gun's loaded and ready."

Yuval stepped on the gas hard and we shot forward.

"Okay, slow down while we observe."

I straightened up in the turret to get a good view of the terrain before we were fully visible. Ahead of me was a wide valley, a uniform brown in color, with ruins of a few houses in a village that had been Syrian up to June 1967. Two miles ahead was the frontier. At first I saw no enemy tanks, then I spied one throwing up a column of exhaust smoke, and behind that a group that was just beginning to move in our direction.

" 'Policeman' stations, on our front, ranges from 500 to 1,500 yards, many enemy tanks. Into position. Open fire! Out."

Having recited the order as I had reviewed it endlessly in maneuvers, I checked that Yair was taking care of the right flank and Ami the left flank. Shells were pouring into the valley, and the Syrians were putting on speed.

"Sir, can we fire?" Gidi requested.

"Okay."

I scanned the valley to see that we had everything covered and that no that Syrians were able to outflank us. Gidi was standing on his chair, peering through field glasses and issuing orders to Kilyon who was traversing the gun accordingly.

"You don't need glasses. There's no time. Fire at them," I yelled at Gidi.

"I have one," Kilyon shouted, "Can I fire?"

"Affirmative, fire!"

Kilyon's gun joined the thunder of the others. The Syrians were still coming, but—as the dust cleared momentarily—Kilyon's target had stopped moving and a Syrian could be seen running from it toward the frontier. Another shell, and the vehicle burst into flames.

"This is the battalion commander. We've caught them with their pants down. We have good positions while they're exposed and on the move. Make use of it! Destroy the lot!"

"Kahalani, this is Yanosh, what's the situation?"

"I'm in contact with Syrians coming from the east towards me."

"You need help?"

"Not at the moment. I'll report later."

The Syrians, their tanks camouflaged with a mix of light and dark green, their cupolas locked down and their commanders out of sight, were spread wide across the landscape. We sat on the ramp and waited for them. Occasionally one of them would stop, fire a shell at us, then start up again. They could see us clearly because our turrets were positioned to allow the guns to fire.

A Syrian was coming straight at my ramp. To my left was Yair Swet, only his head showing above the turret. We ordered our crews to fire, but his was faster. I told mine to hold. Smoke, towering flames. Yair had scored.

Each of our tanks was pounding away as if it were waging a private war, but the Syrians kept coming, directly at Emmy's company. Over near Hermonit, Barzilai and Avi Yahav, commander of Emmy's Number Two Platoon, were firing down a wadi, though not without difficulty since it meant exposing themselves completely to enemy eyes.

Another Syrian was coming straight at us and Yair, but this time I was determined to beat Yair to it.

"Kilyon, have you got the one to our left?"

"No. Can't see it."

I used the traversing handle by my side to bring the turret round.

"Yes. I have him now," Kilyon said, while trying to depress the gun barrel and traverse left simultaneously.

"Fire! He's getting away from us."

"I can't depress enough."

I ordered Yuval to move us forward just enough to tilt the tank down, checking meanwhile that there were no Syrians targetting in on us, but the one we wanted swung in behind a house in the deserted Syrian village, leaving only his aerials visible above the ruins.

"Wait for him. He'll come out the other side. Gideon, have another shell ready."

The tension was tangible. To my left Yair was waiting for the same target. He ordered his gunner to put a shell into the house, but the boy hesitated, so I told Kilyon to do it. A wall crashed down, and the aerials began to move to the left. Slowly the gun came into view, then the turret, then the whole tank.

"Got him? . . . Then give it to him!"

"Somebody already has," Kilyon was disappointed.

Again it was Yair Swet. Even though we hadn't planned it, that was a nice bit of cooperation. We saw the Syrian crew run from their tank into the house. Another shell brought all the walls down, and I put a machine gun burst into the ruins to be sure that we would face no more danger from there.

Emmy stood at the center of his company like an uncaged lion seeking prey. Amnon, still on Booster Ridge with three tanks, was firing phosphor shells at enemy APCs that were bringing up the rear of the armored column. He reported that the Syrians had abandoned their vehicles and were running. Avi Yahav's turrets were just visible near Hermonit. They seemed lonely and far off.

"Battalion commander, Emmy here. We're hitting them and they're burning. I'm under heavy pressure . . . I think you should know—my B2 has gone."

For a moment, I was too busy with the thought that the Syrians could outflank us by way of the wadi to recall who B2 was. Then it flashed into mind. Barzilai. He had been watching the wadi opening till he was killed. The tank was undamaged, and his crew ducked into a deserted bunker to find shelter till the storm passed.

I surveyed our tanks in the entire sector. Our deployment was good, but that wadi on Emmy's front was inviting the Syrians to climb our ridge from under cover. Ami Doron had taken up position to cover the wadi—with Amir Bashari's loader/radioman and gunner still squatting in his turret pannier. Suddenly a shell hit Doron's engine compartment.

By some miracle, the two were not hurt by the impact nor by the intense flame that burst out. They and Doron's crew ran for cover through a hail of artillery fire. Mortar shells were now dropping between the tanks. Boaz Eliav was hit in the eye by a splinter. Doron, who was looking for a substitute tank, took Boaz' place, plugged into the intercom and immediately moved the tank into a firing position.

The Syrians were still coming, apparently determined to get our vantage point. Smoke and flame swirled skyward from points across the terrain. Burning Syrian tanks were exploding and showering chunks of steel across the valley. A turret suddenly shot into the air, landing upside down.

"All 'policemen' stations, this is the battalion commander. You're doing a fine job. This valley looks like a bonfire holiday. Keep firing. It's up to us to stop them."

"Battalion commander, Emmy here. I'm sustaining damage. I need help."

"You'll have it immediately. Yair, this is the battalion commander."

He replied almost instantaneously.

"Leave two platoons where you are, and move with the third to Emmy."

"Confirmed. My deputy will stay on the right flank with two platoons."

"Quickly. I'm with the platoons—and I'll keep an eye on them."

The ever-persistent artillery fire was keeping us buttoned up inside our turrets. About 2,200 yards ahead was the anti-tank ditch, and from the clusters of enemy vehicles we could tell where they had crossed. A bulldozer had filled in sections during the night, and a bridging tank had created another crossing. Snir's guns had worked over the area during the night and seemed to have hit a number of tanks. Now we couldn't tell whether the mass of tanks, half-tracks and APCs was moving—though it didn't particularly worry me for the moment. I was suddenly looking at one of ours—a commanderless tank, outside the ramp.

"This is the battalion commander. Whose tank is that standing above its ramp? I want it back under cover immediately."

No one replied, but it was an open invitation to the Syrians. . . .

"I repeat—whose tank is that? I want it brought down before it gets hit!"

"Emmy here. It's my deputy's. He's gone. The crew has disappeared and there's no one who can bring it down."

Emmy's voice had that tone of frozen sadness which acknowledges the reality of personal loss without having had time to absorb its full impact. Amihai Doron was dead. . . . The tank seemed fine, but he was dead. . . .

"Kahalani. Yanosh here. Report."

"Kahalani here. Am under heavy pressure. Sustaining damage. But I am in position."

"I'm sending help. Returning your deputy to you. Make contact with him!"

"Okay."

Over to my left, one of ours was burning. I couldn't see who, nor did I have time to think about it. The artillery was still pounding us and the Syrians were still coming. Each tank commander was moving up to fire as if to save his life. There was a strange confidence about it that frightened me. Where were they getting this resolve? I knew I could only influence via the radio waves. And I had to keep talking quietly and calmly, as they were used to hearing me.

"Battalion commander, Eitan calling."

"Eitan, you're needed here. Move fast and I'll guide you up to position."

"Happy to be back. I'm coming as fast as I can."

"Brigade commander, Ratess speaking. Seems that a great

many tanks are attacking Kahalani."

Ratess and his battalion were north of the Hermonit.

"Yanosh to Ratess. From which direction are they approaching him?"

"East. He'd better know it."

"Kahalani. Yanosh here. Can you see the force that Ratess is talking about?"

"I'm not clear what he means."

I was worried that maybe he could see more than I had already spotted.

"Yanosh. There are a lot coming at me, but we'll manage."

"In any event, I'm sending you Baruchin."

Baruchin, the assistant brigade operations officer, was in the brigade commander's column with three tanks. He joined us very quickly.

"Brigade commander, Baruchin here. Must send help up here. There are hordes of them coming down the valley."

Yanosh wanted to know how many. I couldn't help thinking that while I had been here alone with half a battalion, everything had gone quietly. Now Baruchin had arrived, he would make everyone tense. We could cope. There was no reason to worry Yanosh, located in the rear.

"Battalion commander, this is Yair's deputy."

Georgi's voice was shaking. He had only been appointed Yair's deputy three months ago and was trying to model himself on his new commander.

"Battalion commander here, go ahead. What's happened?"

"Yair's gone,"he shouted.

How could he be dead? Only minutes before, he had been beside me as we took care of that house down there. Yair had left, with two tanks, to the aid of Emmy. To his left was Yair Carmi from his own company. A shell hit Carmi's tank, but only three men were seen to get out. Daniel Wahnun, the driver, was trapped inside. The flaps over his head wouldn't open— and the fire in the rear compartment was getting worse. Finally, with a superhuman effort, Daniel forced his way out, but was pinned to the ground by artillery fire. The company commander brought his tank close to Carmi's, exposing himself to the Syrian

who had done the damage, then leaned out and down to help
Daniel up. A shell knocked Yair back into the turret. Daniel,
seeing him die, jumped down and ran, screaming, westward
towards our lines. Yair Lipschitz, the gunner, and his loader/
radioman were both wounded—one in the chest, the other in
the leg. Shocked by the sight of Yair Swet's corpse, they jumped
out and joined Daniel's mad flight.

"Georgi, this is the battalion commander. Take over the
company."

The number of shells ready for firing is always limited, and
tanks have to retire from the action to transfer ammunition from
their bellies. They were doing it one after the other and racing
back to firing positions. The Syrians were still coming, and the
fact that the damage to their comrades didn't stop them was
worrying me. Could they be that brave? Hard to believe. My
men had courage, and I wasn't exactly among the cowards—
but I would have slowed down my advance in such conditions
and would have leapfrogged from cover to cover. Now it was
getting difficult to tell which of the tanks in the valley had been
abandoned and which were still functional war machines. More
serious, many of our tanks were being hit by Syrians standing
among trees or ruined buildings and sniping. Right now I could
see one of that variety about 800 yards away among the trees.
Swinging the gun round, I gave a fire order.

"I can't see him," Kilyon shouted.

"It's becoming a habit. Try hard—left of the trees."

"A moment . . . I think I see him."

I waited impatiently till he confirmed and fired. Gideon loaded
a fresh shell while Kilyon marked the previous one.

"Yanosh stations, this is the deputy brigade commander. Fuel
and ammunition are available at the rear road junction."

"Battalion commander, this is Amnon," the voice cut while I
was supervising the gunnery.

"Gidi, you carry on firing . . . Amnon, battalion commander
here."

"Enemy APCs trying to approach Booster Ridge. I'm trying
to hit them."

"Short. Raise two-thousandths," Gidi said to Kilyon.

"Battalion commander here. I can see your tanks firing. Remember! Your positions are particularly important—as a long-range observation post."

"Firing," Kilyon announced as another shell winged on its way. While waiting for Amnon to respond, I watched the field.

"Getting low on ammunition," Amnon said. "I'll have to send a tank back to fill up."

The last shell was right next to the Syrian. I saw the crew jump out and run.

"Hold on, Amnon," I said into the mike, then switched to intercom. "Gidi, leave that one. The crew's gone. Pity to waste shells." And to spoil a good tank that we can collect after the war, I added to myself.

"Amnon, I don't want any tanks pulling back now. We need them all."

"Battalion commander, Emmy here. My Number One Platoon leader has had it."

Boaz Freedman had only come to us two months before, after pestering Armor School to release him from instructor duties and return him to a field unit. I asked how it had happened.

"He was in Amir's spot covering the wadi. . . . "

"Battalion commander, Eitan here."

"Eitan, go ahead, over."

"I've arrived. I'm to your right."

Glancing in his direction, I saw that Eitan was in the turret of another tank—not his own.

"How many have you brought?"

"Two reduced platoons."

The third platoon of Menahem's company from Quneitra had joined Yair Nafshi, a lieutenant-colonel who was covering our forward position below Booster Ridge. Meanwhile, Dr. Alex was still at Waset Junction, hungry for news and trying to understand the radio traffic. One of Menahem's tank commanders turned up with a bullet through his neck and was promptly cross-examined by the medical team. Kobi, the communications officer, had taken a command car on a rescue mission into Quneitra. At Ein Zivan he pulled up, wondering whether to risk the bombardment on the road in an unprotected vehicle, then decided he must continue. Racing through the hail of shrapnel, he picked up crews that were left with abandoned and damaged tanks, and headed back down the road—on three good wheels and a flat caused by shell splinters.

"Battalion commander, Emmy here. The Syrians are trying to break through my company."

"Any point you can't control?"

"No. I just wanted you to know."

Eitan detached some tanks to support Emmy.

"Sir, we must drop back to transfer shells from the belly to the turret," Gidi told me.

As we loaded, I surveyed the battalion. The tanks no longer looked ready for review, as they had this morning. Outside equipment boxes were ripped by shrapnel. On Emmy's sector one of ours was burning. Another had been abandoned, with its gun pointing skyward. The commanders were tired and tense. Ammunition stocks were dwindling. Officers were dying, and each and every one was now fighting for his life.

A tank passed by on its way to Emmy. I tried to identify the commander. As if in answer to my unspoken wish, he pulled up alongside me. I recognized Avinoam Shemesh under the dust and grime, and pointed in the direction of the ramp, 200 yards to the northeast. He waved, then smiled in reply to my thumbs-up blessing.

Most of the Syrian advance was contained. I knew we had succeeded. Their fire from individual tanks was now desperate as they tried to save their own lives. Here and there we could see crew members running towards the border, leaving behind tanks, some of which seemed to be in good condition. We would use them later. For the time being, we had stopped them.

Dr. Alex got an urgent call to evacuate a serious casualty. Sass, his sergeant-major, took a half-track to the tank lines, even though the armorer officer stopped him en route to tell him he wouldn't get through the bombardment. Eitan guided him in next to a tank, the cupola of which was stained with blood. He had come for Avinoam Shemesh—but Avinoam no longer needed evacuation. Meanwhile, another casualty—not of our battalion— was brought in to Alex for treatment. He asked the doctor whether there was any news of his best friend—Avinoam Shemesh. No, as far as Alex knew, everything was okay. Then the man, Second Lieutenant Shmid, was put on a command car that was to take

him to the hospital. The sergeant-major drove in with Avinoam's
body, covered by a blanket. After hesitating for a few moments,
Dr. Alex finally decided that Shmid would have to share the
ride to the rear with his dead friend.

"Kahalani. Yanosh here. What's happening?"

"We've stopped them. It's quite a sight. The valley is full of
burning and abandoned hardware."

"Can you estimate numbers?"

"Well, if you don't accuse me of a fertile imagination, I guess
we've hit eighty or ninety."

I remembered that during the Six-Day War some tank commanders had exaggerated numbers of hits, creating the impres-
sion of a bigger enemy force than actually existed. Then again,
there was the War of Attrition, when a bottle of champagne was
given to any crew that hit an enemy tank. We could bathe in
champagne this time.

"Good. Good."

"Brigade commander, we have to think of rearming and
refueling."

"Stay where you are. Another unit may come in to relieve
you."

"Confirm. Over and out."

What unit would that be? Though we had neither the time
nor the inclination to know what was going on elsewhere, I
understood that Ben-Shoham was having troubles of his own
on the southern sector.

"Planes! Planes!"

Hearing the cry over the battalion net, I looked up to see two
MiGs coming in on us. Feeling helpless, I ducked down in the
turret and waited for the bombs to fall. But they passed overhead
with a maddening slowness, giving us a full view of their un-
derwing armament, made a wide circle—then headed back in
our direction. I loaded my 0.3 machine gun. Right down the
line, tank commanders were firing. The Syrians swept over in
complete confidence and let their loads drop. The black objects,
looking like barrels, twisted and turned eastward. Again I ducked
and waited. The seconds seemed like hours. A tremendous explosion—and I lifted my head to see a cloud of billowing smoke
and dust 100 yards behind us. No hit even though there was

nothing to hamper them. But where was our Air Force? I was angry. I didn't intend to battle planes, too. That was not my job. We had always been promised that the Air Force would take care of the sky, but we hadn't seen them for two days.

"Brigade commander, Kahalani here. I've just been attacked by enemy aircraft."

"Yanosh here. I saw."

"Can't we have air to take care of them—and on those blasted crossings at the ditch?"

"I'll deal with it."

Yanosh sounded worried. Syrian tank penetrations occurred to the north in the area of Buka'ta and Hermonit, where Ratess was deployed. He had been attacked by a smaller number of tanks than the force that came at me. But then he had his own problems: hills to the south and lower hillocks covered with fruit trees and grapevines. His force had to be split into small groups to cope with every possible opening. And the terrain was ideal for infantry, who could approach his tanks without being seen. Apart from that, Ratess didn't have time to get organized. He did not even have a tank of his own. He was controlling the battle from a Jeep. In fact, there was a moment when it annoyed me. Ratess was no less senior that Yanosh, and it was no more than a chain of strange coincidences that gave one command over the other. Yet it didn't seem to be causing any tension. Occasionally I heard Gideon Weiler, Ratess' deputy, on the net. I hoped Gideon was being careful. His family suffered enough when Adam fell.

I scoured the area, trying to identify the cause of the cloud of dust beyond Khan Areinbe: was it from tanks, APCs or trucks? I decided to prepare for the worst—more tanks. Meanwhile, the artillery were pounding us again, with deadly precision. Shrapnel pattered on the hull, and I couldn't help thinking how badly off we would be without our steel protection. I remembered my father telling me as a child that the ones to be scared of weren't the shells that whistled. They passed on. The dangerous ones were those you didn't hear.

There was no point in standing and waiting to be decimated. I poked my head out to check which tanks I would leave in place and which I would withdraw. I decided on three of Yair's tanks for the right sector, and three of Emmy's for the left, and gave orders accordingly.

"Battalion commander, Emmy here. A tank is firing at us all the time."

"Where is he?"

"Among the rocks in the wadi."

I couldn't see him from where I was, but I could guess from the direction of Emmy's fire.

"Why can't you get him?"

"The tank that shoots him must be fully exposed."

The Centurion gun had an advantage in low-shoot capabilities—a depression of nine degrees as against five for the Russian-built T-55—but that wouldn't help shooting downhill.

"Work slowly and carefully. I don't want any of ours hurt."

"I'm moving into position. Don't worry."

Where did he get his strength? Most of his officers were dead, but he was still sounding vigorous and confident. Right through training, he had been brainwashing his company into believing they were the best. But now the artillery bombardment on his boys was worrying me.

"What's happening?"

"I'll have the bastard in a moment."

"Emmy, seems to me that he's fighting for his life. I would prefer to leave him be for a few minutes and let his crew run for it. No need to take risks over one idiot."

"Sir, give me one more minute. I'll destroy him."

Emmy and another tank started by Hermonit used a technique whereby one fired while the other marked the shots. Kilyon and Gideon meanwhile used the lull to transfer shells from the tank belly. Gidi told me that he was preparing armor-piercing and hollow charge shells that would be more useful against tanks. The armor-piercing has the highest velocity and therefore stands a better chance of scoring hits. The hollow charge is double purpose: against armor and "soft-skinned" targets, including infantry.

"Battalion commander, this is Emmy. I got the son of a bitch. He's burning."

There were still tanks and APCs to be seen down by the anti-tank ditch—some damaged and others abandoned—and the Syrians could possibly get them out during the night. We hadn't tried our hand at long-range shooting so far, but no Syrian tank was going to get away if I could help it. The crews were ordered to pick their own targets. Soon more "bonfires" were added to the scene.

"Battalion commander here. What about rearming?"

Eitan, my deputy, replied, "I've taken care of it. We've got shells and fuel beyond the crossing. You can send tanks. Over."

He was talking about the main road crossing between Qunei-tra—Bukata and Gonen—Damascus.

"I'll send you three at a time."

"Okay."

It was already noon. The temperature outside was high, and inside the tanks the air was even hotter. We were all in coveralls and hadn't stepped out of the tanks for a full twenty-four hours, not even to answer the calls of nature. Since the bombardment had eased, crew members were permitted out in turns with instructions not to move far from the tanks. I didn't want anyone hit by shrapnel. Our fireproof coveralls were comfortable but thin, and difficult to put on and take off. I sent the tanks back in turn to refuel and rearm, while all the others remained in firing positions. I picked up a map and identified the valley through which the Syrian tanks had come. No name. Well, I could name it for our battalion. The brigade operations officer cut into my thoughts.

"Yanosh wants a meeting with you."

18

OCTOBER 7, 1973   AFTERNOON/NIGHT

We decided to have it at the crossing. I summoned Eitan back
to battalion and took my vehicle down to the crossing. Yanosh
arrived in an APC, accompanied by Haggai, the operations officer; Ilan, his intelligence officer; and Shalom, his signals officer.
All four seemed tired. They were unshaven and their eyes were
bloodshot. I jumped down, taking a map and helmet. I must
have been a sight—covered in dust and tank grease, my windbreaker a few sizes too big, grimy overalls, without rank insignia.
Yanosh smiled and we shook hands. I was proud of what the
battalion had done this morning, and I could see some of it
reflected in Yanosh's eyes.

"Come on, let's sit down. How do you feel?"

"Fine."

I felt four pairs of eyes studying me as we found a place to
sit by the roadside. "Kahalani, you've done excellent work. My
compliments to you and your men."

"I've lost a lot of them."

"I know . . . I want you to know that the Syrians aren't finished
with this. They have enough tanks and they'll try to break through
again."

Were we going to go through that all over again?

Yanosh asked for a map.

"They have two possibilities on our sector. One—to try again
at the same place. Two—and it's more reasonable—to break
through Quneitra and the area south of the town."

Yanosh was marking arrows on the map as he spoke.

"I find it hard to believe," I said, "that they will come through
the valley again. It takes a lot of courage to pass between damaged and burned-out tanks."

"You're right, but we must be prepared for it nevertheless. Finish rearming. I want you to stay in the same place for tonight."

"I'm in the middle of rearming now. I would like to bring Amnon down from Bustar. He's not effective up there, and I need his tanks."

"The ridge is important. We can't leave it."

"Yair Nafshi is to the east of it with his tanks. He can stop the Syrians from taking the ridge."

I knew Yanosh couldn't refuse me. Apart from Amnon and Emmy, I had no company commanders. Yair Swet was dead. Menahem was injured. And Zamir had been taken as a brigade tactical reserve. I needed Amnon.

"Alright, Kahalani, take him. Haggai, inform Yair Nafshi that we're pulling Amnon off Bustar, and that he is now responsible for the sector."

"Incidentally," I asked, "what about support forces?"

There had been a conversation between Yanosh and Raphael Eitan, the division commander, over the radio this morning. Mention had been made of reserves.

"Not at this stage. The southern sector has trouble. The Syrians broke through and made some ground. All the effort is going in there."

We shook hands and he climbed back on the APC. Before joining him, Haggai hugged me.

"You were great, my friend."

I drove to the battalion refueling point. Trucks were dotted across the field, and the tanks were standing beside them loading shells directly. Reservists were helping to open the crates. The method of loading necessitated swivelling the turret from time to time as the loader/radioman accepted shells for different compartments. Drivers were checking their engines while the other crew members took on iron rations for the next twenty-four hours.

The sheer density of vehicles worried me. They were all in a hurry to load the tanks—but no one was paying any attention to security and the possibility of air attack. Gidi directed our tank in alongside an ammunition truck and began, together with Kilyon and Gideon, to load shells. Yuval went off to get food. I sat down on a rock and studied the map again. I was very tired and, for a moment, troubled by the thought that I wasn't helping my crew to load. But I knew I needed some time to myself to absorb what had happened and to plan the next moves. I was looking for a suitable place to deploy against any invasion via Quneitra. Suddenly, shouts and soldiers running in every direction. Without thinking, I ran, and arrived at the tank puffing and blowing.

"What happened, Gidi?"

The battalion operations officer was standing in his compartment, studying the sky.

"Planes."

"Where?"

"Don't know. Someone shouted."

"Yuval, start your engine and move out."

So, I thought, my premonition was right—and now we had to be clear of all that ammunition.

"Halt!" I shouted as I grabbed for the machine gun.

Two MiGs were coming in low from the east. The air was full of 0.3 bullets, much of them being fired too low for my liking, but the tanks strewn across this field weren't mine, and there was nothing I could do about it. The MiGs passed low overhead, taking no notice of us, swung southwest and dropped their bombs on Quneitra. I stayed on the tank while the crew finished loading.

On the way back to our positions, I could see tanks coming in to rears from all the sectors—but I could also see heavy shellfire on the road. The Syrians knew it was our main traffic route. I could also see shells falling on our positions. We swung off across a field to approach the position from the rear. There was a huge explosion. Looking upwards, I saw two parachutes moving slowly earthwards, perhaps 500 yards from me. Their burning plane seemed to be coming down right on us. Ordering Yuval to stop, I ducked inside the turret and waited for the crash. It wasn't long in coming. The earth shook. A big black crater had opened up not far from us. Sticking out of it was the remains of a wing, with Israeli Air Force markings. But the wind was westerly, and the parachutes of the Phantom's crew were being carried to the east. There was no time to waste.

"All 'policeman' stations, battalion commander here. Stand

by to pick up the two pilots. They might drop near us and must be picked up at any price."

Eitan and Amnon confirmed.

"Yuval, step on it."

The parachutes continued down till they dropped from sight to the east.

"Battalion commander, Eitan here. It's okay, we have one of the pilots, and the other will be collected immediately."

One of the pilots dropped in our lines. The other was a little to the east. An APC went out and got him under cover of the tank guns. Both were taken to the rear at speed.

As the artillery bombardment died down, I ordered all the damaged tanks to be towed down from the ramps so that Dr. Alex could remove the dead and the fitters could start repairs. Yair's was among the first to go. It could be driven, but we were afraid of some damage to the steering mechanism—and Yair's body was still inside. Word of his death was relayed to Alex, who took his medical orderlies to get the body. It wasn't easy. They had to traverse the turret and raise the gun—work for which the medicos had never been trained. After listing the tank number, and marking the body for identification—since Yair's dogtags had been torn off—Alex was informed by Emmy about Ami Doron, whose tank was still in position. Alex brought his command car up the ramp and transferred the body, then sent both off to the hospital at Safad.

A little later, Eitan met with Alex and the other two officers—the armorer and signaller. They were complaining about not being properly integrated in the battalion line-up. Alex emphasized that he wasn't mobile enough with only one half-track. Eitan ruled that the armorer officer's APC should also be at his disposal.

On Emmy's sector, I noticed a tank out of position and exposed. I asked him to check. He reported back that it seemed abandoned, though its engine was running.

"Make sure you're covered, and take a look inside."

Through my field glasses, I watched Emmy climb up and waited tensely for him to report. Maybe someone was sitting inside, wounded and screaming. Emmy peered into the turret and the driver's compartment, then returned to his own tank.

"It's Amir Bashari's tank," he said in the tones of a man expecting a reprimand.

"Are you sure?"

"Amir's sitting inside with an ammunition box in his hands."

"How did the tank get there?"

"The driver must have got this far last night."

"Where is he?"

"The flaps are open. He's gone."

I ordered them to look for him, though not much could be done. The thought that one of my men was missing wasn't pleasant. Maybe he had been taken prisoner?

Late afternoon. In the last light of a sun sinking behind our backs, we tried to spot enemy movements to the east. Down below in the valley, the smashed and blackened Syrian hulks stood as memorials to their crews. In our territory, and across the border, there was no one to be seen, no vehicle moving— only an eerie silence, broken by an occasional shell dropping on volcano Avital behind us, and south of Hermonit.

All the tanks were refueled, rearmed and ready for a new battle. I split the force into two companies, one under Emmy— composed of tanks from other companies—and the other under Amnon, with the tanks from Booster Ridge. Amnon had increased his force using Emmy's technique; Menahem's company no longer existed, his tank commanders having been sent to the two companies in search of new leadership. Georgi was commanding four tanks from Yair's company. Eitan slotted in. Laor— straight from prison and complete with one tank—joined Georgi's force.

I rearranged the deployment, assigning sectors to each company commander and making sure that the tanks were prepared for the night. Then my thoughts turned to the men who had died. I wondered whether the Syrians would attack during the night and, if so, how—would it be tanks or bazooka crews? Were my tanks in the best places to cope with any kind of attack? Then, it hit me . . . hunger.

"Hey, don't we get anything to eat in this crate?"

"You're hungry?" Kilyon asked in feigned astonishment.

"A few more minutes and you won't have me here at all. I'm starving to death."

"Okay. We'll open an iron ration. Can we get out?"

"Yes, but quickly."

Anyone outside could hold us up if we needed to act fast. Gideon cut a slice of meat loaf and slapped it on to hardtack crackers together with a pickled cucumber. It made a good meal. The canteen passed from hand to hand to wash down the dry crackers.

The moon appeared in full regalia. All was silence except for the occasional clatter of an engine cowling being slid back in place. The drivers, well aware of what might happen, were checking their machines thoroughly. From the engines, they moved to the tracks and shock absorbers.

"Kahalani. Haggai here. Be ready for bazooka teams as well as tanks. Over."

"Just let them try it."

I instructed the battalion to test their machine guns, aiming east, both to be sure that the weapons were functioning and to remind the men that infantry with bazookas were also a possibility.

We were on stand-by till eleven at night, but nothing happened. The Syrians fired an occasional star shell, yet all was quiet. Amnon, whose tank was next to mine, came over to join me. We sat in silence for a while, then he asked whether we had been given a new task.

"At the moment, there's still work to be done here. When we finish, they'll take care of us."

"Did you see how we hit the Syrians that tried to climb Booster?"

"You did good work. How many tanks have you got now?"

"Eight. Perhaps the fitters will repair one more."

"Battalion comander. Emmy here."

"Yes."

"Edri was killed, but it's not certain that his body was evacuated."

What the hell was this? Strange report to receive now! I asked for details.

"He was killed during the morning, but no one had time . . ."

"Then how do you know he was killed and not wounded?"

"Ofer saw him hit by Syrian machine-gun fire after he jumped from his tank."

"Is Ofer certain?"

"Yes. During the day it wasn't possible to get near him because the Syrians were waiting for anything that moved there."

"Can anyone get to his tank now?"

"It means going down into the wadi."

"Then I prefer to wait till morning. I hope that your information is correct."

In battle there was no time for casualty reports. Tank comrades saw the hits on their comrades, but didn't—couldn't—spare time to watch their neighbors. We were all on the firing line, all fighting a personal battle for life or death. Edri was one of us on the line.

Alive to the danger of attack by bazooka teams, we settled down to wait out the night. Two men stayed awake in every tank. Removing my helmet, I sat in the command seat and tried to sleep. Radio messages woke me from time to time. I wasn't relaxed enough. Perhaps something had been overlooked, something I should have done to protect my tanks. Outside, the night was cold. Inside, the heat was pleasant yet not conducive to the sleeplessness that my turn on watch required. From time to time, I splashed water on my face.

19

OCTOBER 8, 1973   DAY

Dawn. The hum of tank engines grew in intensity as the crews warmed up their machines and made their routine checks. Rays of sunlight pierced the dark, illuminating the black shapes visible during the night and revealing them to be trees, dwellings and rocks. We moved into firing positions. When I was sure that there was no suspicious movement on the terrain, I ordered the engines turned off.

The sky turned grey and rain poured down, soaking the layer of dust that had settled on the tanks. It's raining, I thought, and I hadn't finished fixing the roof on my house. The furniture would get wet. But what did it matter? The only important thing now was to get home in one piece. Anyway, I could rely on Dalia. Perhaps my father had already fixed it. What nonsense! The whole of Israel was mobilized and at war, and here I was, worrying about furniture. We could always buy new. Wonder where Emanuel is? Perhaps in Sinai on a Patton. I hoped he wouldn't be rash. In the War of Attrition, his battalion commander complained that he wasn't cautious enough. I smiled at the thought. Emanuel—never walking, always running! Arnon was in my battalion with a technical crew. I didn't know whether anybody had been hurt in the rear. I thought of asking the armorer officer, then decided that I didn't want to know. Better that way. . . .

The rain would help our containment battle. Mud would force the Syrians to move on well-defined tracks—but this morning's rain wasn't enough. The crews made the best of the lull to have a good meal. Gideon opened iron rations and we all ate our fill.

In the Valley of Death below, we could see the Syrians standing exactly as they had been at sunset yesterday. There had been no attempt to tow them off.

Yanosh asked for a situation report. Everything seemed quiet.

"Be ready to move up to the frontier to sweep the area," he cautioned.

I ordered the men into their compartments ready to move. While they took their places, I mapped out our descent into the valley, ensuring full cover.

"Report when ready to move," Yanosh said.

"Ready, over."

"Then start a sweep, but be careful of an ambush."

About 2,750 yards separated us from the frontier. The engines growled and Amnon moved forward, close alongside, to the road then up a low ridge 330 yards ahead. Eitan and Emmy stayed in position to cover Amnon's company and me. There was some hesitancy about the descent from the ramps. We could no longer see the entire valley stretched out below—and we were exposed. Shells began to fall between the tanks. The fire was so accurate that I for a moment believed it had to be from direct sighting. We ducked into our turrets and tried, with the help of field glasses, to pinpoint the source of fire. Amnon took a position and was ready to cover Emmy, whose tanks now began to move at my command. They slid down the slope and spread out among the ruins of the village that had been beneath us. It wasn't long before they were also treated to a hail of artillery fire.

"Those creeps start early in the morning. Gidi, see if you can spot where it's coming from," I said into the intercom.

We were both outside the cupolas. He put glasses to his eyes, but had no luck. I radioed Mizrahi, the brigade support officer, and asked him to try to locate the guns that were firing at us—then silence them. He said they would try. We moved on slowly, keeping a watch in all directions. I was particularly concerned about the tanks through which we were passing. Some Syrian crewman might still be inside waiting to fire at us. The artillery was getting closer. Shrapnel winged overhead, occasionally rattling on our armor. Emmy's tanks moved blithely through the hail.

"Battalion commander here. All 'policeman' stations, watch

out for the artillery. I don't want any unnecessary risks. Remember, our main task is to sweep the area clear of enemy. And be careful of the tanks you pass."

I kept my eyes on gun barrels—ready for surprises in this steel graveyard.

"Amnon here. Up front, south of Tel Dahur, I can see enemy machines. They seem to be firing missiles at Emmy."

"Hold on."

I had them now. APCs in position and firing missiles at a frequency of a few minutes apart.

"Amnon. Try to hit them."

In parallel, I told Gidi to prepare to fire. Missiles. The first time I was encountering them. We couldn't see them in flight, but they were hitting near the tanks. Later, I could see them coming at us, but we couldn't spot the source. Amnon fired at the APCs, but they were too low down. It was a waste of shells. They were BRDM missile-carrying armored cars. We hadn't seen them in the Six-Day War. I glanced over at Emmy's force. Two tanks were pulling back, one chained to the other.

"Eitan, what's going on over there?"

"One tank hit. We're pulling it back from firing position."

"Can it be fixed if you find a lower spot?"

"Negative."

"Then take it back to where we were this morning."

As I watched the progress of the tow, another of Emmy's tanks was hit—by an artillery shell on the engine. Its commander, First Sergeant Zelig Haberman, was killed by shrapnel. After checking that Zelig was indeed dead, the crew jumped out and into a neighboring tank. The damaged vehicle was towed out. We stopped 550 yards from the ditch. From there we could clearly see Syrian tanks and the two crossings they prepared on Yom Kippur night, plus an overturned bridge which I guessed hadn't been installed because its crew was hit. Perhaps that was Snir's doing.

Yanosh was watching from Booster Ridge, and I could hear Raful, the division commander, asking him to continue the sweep and be prepared to hold this line overnight. A red light flashed in my mind. It would be tragic to stay near the border for the sake of holding flat, exposed land without prepared positions.

And it would need more tanks than I had at my disposal. Yanosh finished talking with Raful and ordered me to be prepared to establish a defense line on the spot. I decided on attack.

"Where I'm standing is lousy for defense. Yanosh, I need a larger force and the fire positions are bad. Where I was yesterday is much better. Up there we have a bottleneck through which the enemy has to come to us. I suggest that we make that our base for the night."

"Okay. I accept your reasoning. When you finish the sweep, choose your own place."

Emmy tried to hitch his own tank to Zelig's but wasn't successful. It was taking too long, and we could see dust rising around Khan Areinbe. If those were approaching tanks, we were in a lousy spot to meet them. I ordered a move back to our previous positions. It was slow and careful going. Zelig's tank stayed in the valley. We would collect it later.

While we were sweeping the valley, Alex at Waset Junction had a visitor—Major Yona Teren, who had been a deputy battalion commander in the brigade some two years back. He asked if Alex knew where I was, and the doctor promptly offered him the APC radio.

"Battalion commander, Yona here, over."

The voice sounded strange. For a moment I thought it must be a call sign of a new unit that had arrived.

"Who called?"

"Yona here."

"Who's Yona?"

I go through this often. People coming up to me and asking enthusiastically how I am and so on—and I just don't place them or remember who they are. Yona offered a few details about himself, then asked impatiently to join me.

"Alright, but you'll have to be quick. I don't think it will last more than three days. Still there's a lot to do, so grab a tank and come along."

After some argument with Alex, who knew what was happening up ahead, Yona finally persuaded the doctor to let him take the APC up to our positions. They set out, Yona in command, according to Alex's instructions. Suddenly Yona bellowed: "Halt, reverse fast!" The astonished medical team peered out of the APC to see a Syrian tank 50 yards away. Yona had taken a wrong road and ended up near the frontier. Keeping his head, he directed the APC into cover, then after a few minutes of tension and anxiety, got them out of there.

Alex had some wounded to collect from Emmy's company. When they arrived, Yona jumped into a tank from which the wounded crew had been evacuated. The casualties on board the APC told Alex that Zelig, their commander, was still lying dead in his tank. Alex radioed Eitan for permission to go and get him but was told to wait till the bombardment slackened off. The truth was that none of us was happy about leaving the tank out there.

Yona reported that he was now part of the force and ready for action. He joined Emmy's company as a single tank—but I knew that I would be adding more vehicles to him as time went on. Couldn't waste that experience and know-how! I made a note to myself to beware of offending Yona's sensibilities. He was a classmate, and all the company officers were much younger.

There was tension in the air. Inside Syrian territory we could see tanks moving, but the direction wasn't clear. We were in firing position when I heard Second Lieutenant Avi Yahav, Emmy's Number Two Platoon commander. He was excited—and I wasn't used to hearing platoon officers on that frequency.

"Ten Syrian tanks approaching."

I straightened up in the turret and surveyed the valley, but saw nothing.

"Which direction?"

"Straight at us."

"Alright, be ready to fire. I'll reinforce you."

Hearing the exchange over the radio, the whole battalion snapped to alert. Minutes passed and I still saw nothing. It was beginning to irritate me. Then I asked Avi the question I should perhaps have asked in the beginning.

"What range are they?"

"Five or six kilometers."

"Then why are you driving me crazy? You couldn't have said so at first? At that range, I'm not interested."

I didn't normally issue reprimands over the radio, but Avi had caused unnecessary tension in the battalion.

In the late afternoon, Lieutenant-Colonel Yos Eldar returned from the hospital. Actually, he "escaped" from the hospital, seeing no point in remaining there. Arriving at Yanosh's head-quarters, he boarded an APC, collected a few tanks and came up to us, intending to let us withdraw to reorganize and rest. I gave him a quick briefing on the sector and its problems, then pulled out. Nothing had changed at the improvised supply base. Hordes of trucks filled the narrow area, while others on the road made tank movement difficult. Amnon's company stayed be-hind with Yos. In the supply area were Eitan with what remained of Yair's company, three tanks under Georgi's command and Emmy's small force.

I jumped off the tank to stretch my legs. Officers from brigade who were in charge of the refueling base came over. The brigade quartermaster inquired whether I was in need of anything spe-cial. Apart from hollow charge shells, I requested batteries for the infrascopes, our eyes at night. He said he would try. Sachs, the brigade armorer, joined the conversation, his 6-foot 8-inch frame towering over us.

"Kahalani, I hear that you really gave it to them."

I smiled. He realized that this wasn't the time for pleasantries and informed me that his teams were standing by in force to look after my damaged tanks.

"Alright, I don't know what you'll do, but I want more tanks at any price. Even if it means working on repairs round the clock. And make sure you send me tanks with crews."

"I can promise you repaired tanks, but I don't know how we'll man them."

"You'll collect them. I rely on you."

My crew was loading up. I studied the map, hoping we would have a few hours in the rear. We were all tired and tense, and a rest would do us good. But it was not to be. On the brigade frequency, I heard Lientenant-Colonel Yair report, from Position Seven on the line, that large numbers of Syrians were moving towards us. I didn't wait for orders from Yanosh, but ordered my crews back into their tanks and to be ready for immediate movement. Then I ran a head count and found that Yona had vanished. I called him on the radio, and he answered that he was looking for a number of tanks to command. Probably he hadn't felt comfortable without responsibility and a chance to use his experience. Anyway, I promised him a number of tanks and a company command, and he came back to us. Yanosh came through with orders to proceed to the border and block a Syrian advance.

"What area?"

"Move fast to Forward Position Nine, and stop them there," Yanosh said, referring to a point south of Quneitra on a ridge that we held.

We weren't all ready, but I knew the best way to speed it up was to start moving myself. I rolled slowly down the line of refueling and rearming tanks, waving and shouting at the astonished men to get moving. The ones who were refueling from tankers dropped the diesel oil nozzles and jumped into their compartments. On other tanks, men standing over the engines stowed the last shell and climbed into place. Within minutes we were rolling. Over the radio, I was asked where we were going. The reply, "Follow me. I'll explain on the way."

My tank raced down the road to Quneitra, followed by Eitan, Emmy, Georgi and three more tanks under the command of Zamir—though I had no idea how he had joined us and at whose command. Hundreds of Syrian shells were falling on the town, causing pillars of smoke to shroud the town. I was well aware that we must not enter because of a possible trap. To our right, Tel Avital was taking a pounding no lighter than that at Quneitra. I reckoned that they were out to destroy the communication antennas on top of the hill.

I took the battalion across the fields of Ein Zivan and Merom Golan, between the two concentrations of fire. I tried hard not to do damage, holding to an avenue of trees as long as I could, but this was no time for parade-ground niceties. We had to move fast and in a wide line so that as many tanks as possible would come straight into firing positions. Nevertheless, I was sorry when I rolled over an irrigation pipe that lay in our path. Emmy drew alongside as we raced in parallel, both ready to fire.

Over the battalion frequency, I gave details on where we were going and why. We could already see Position Nine. The sun was sinking, and Tel Avital cast a long, narrow shadow. I decided to deploy on the steep ridges north of the position. Below them we could already see damaged and abandoned Syrian tanks—the ones that Zamir had hit on Yom Kippur night as they tried to break into Kibbutz Ein Zivan.

Taking position was complicated. Apart from the slope, we had to keep clear of minefields that surrounded our forward position. I moved down a narrow track, the others following me. On top, I took a look at the Syrian terrain. There were tanks far away. The sun was behind us, and it wasn't difficult to watch the Syrians. There were perhaps fifteen, though more might have been out of sight.

An hour later, I knew that the reports were not correct. Fifteen tanks were not particularly worrisome. We fired at them, but the range was too great. Avraham Snir reported that the Air Force had been requested to deal with them. Our tanks were clearly marked with yellow panels, so we were sure our pilots could identify us. But suddenly a plane dived and dropped its bombs on the tanks to my right. Swinging round to make sure there were no more, I called Yanosh.

Haggai answered in Yanosh's name.

"Our own air is attacking us. Get them off. I'll manage without them."

"I'll stop them immediately. Where are you?"

"A little north of Position Nine, on the ridges."

The Syrians were stopped a long way from our positions. Probably they wouldn't attack while the sun was still in their eyes. On the other hand, I was not comfortable at that spot. We were on a slope so steep that the tanks had to sit on the very peak in order to fire. Eitan and the two deputy company commanders were in position around our strongpoint below, because there wasn't room for all of us up top. I spent the last few minutes before sunset mentally marking points that I might need for navigation during the night.

20

OCTOBER 8, 1973   NIGHT

As day turned to night, I tried to reassure Yanosh that I could not see any movement in our direction apart from the fifteen tanks. I added that I did not think they would come during the night because of the difficult terrain. Then I got an order to leave a small force at Position Nine, and to take the rest as reserve for Yos, whose tanks were still in position facing "the Vale of Tears," as we were calling our valley. I moved out slowly, followed by Emmy, leaving Eitan to hold the ridge. The route was made difficult by the dark and because we had to bypass Quneitra.

"Head for the crossing," Yanosh ordered.

"I am. We'll stand somewhere nearby. There are light showers here," I said, referring to phosphor shells that were falling on the crossroads, illuminating the area in eerie white and shooting burning chemical in every direction.

"Are they firing at you?"

"The area," I replied, careful not to be precise in case the Syrians were listening to our frequency. I was wondering whether they had observers on the ground to direct their fire. We moved north onto the road to our valley and waited a few minutes. Again the shells dropped, illuminating the whole area.

I heard Yos shouting, begging for star shells. Just like Yom Kippur night. Yanosh's intervention didn't help. There were no star shells. I couldn't attempt to estimate the force attacking him, but I very much wanted to join him. I knew how badly off he was for manpower, tanks and illumination, and here we were standing idly at the crossroads. Feeling our fatigue, we deployed for night camp.

Yanosh asked about the situation at Position Nine. Eitan reported all quiet, and I relayed the information to brigade.

"Transfer your deputy to the brigade frequency and tell him to move fast to aid Yos."

I passed on Yanosh's instruction, noting the excitement in Eitan's voice at the thought of action. Very soon his force passed us on its way to the Vale of Tears.

"Brigade commander, Kahalani here. Do you see the situation in Quneitra?" I drew attention to the flares and artillery shells being dropped on Quneitra, the Golan's largest town, by Syrian planes.

"Yes. We'll wait a while."

It seemed to me that they were staging a well-planned attack, in which a stream of armor would come through the town and head north—towards us.

"Yanosh, I suggest that we move nearer and place a block to the north of the town."

"Alright. But under no conditions are you to go in."

"I'll stay to the north."

He repeated the instruction, though I had no intention of getting caught in that fire trap. I didn't even know who controlled the town. The wild roar of engines shook the fatigue out of us as we began to move southward, Snir and Emmy close alongside me. Major Yona slipped into Emmy's column. The darkness didn't help. Yuval almost slipped off the road a number of times, and Gidi had to guide him all the way. One track slid into the drainage ditch by the roadside, and we almost overturned. Suddenly I saw ahead a wider strip of water and yelled to pull up fast. He did, almost at the last moment. While I was yelling at him, I heard engine noise behind and turned to see Snir's tank racing down on us.

"Snir, stop," I screamed into the radio. But he kept on coming. I ducked down in the turret, already thinking about which tank I would have to take to replace my own. Snir banged into us with a heavy thud. I lifted my head to see his gun barrel across my turret, exactly where my head had been a moment before.

"Emmy, battalion commander here. Stop immediately!"

"I've stopped."

Emmy's column braked to a halt.

"Gidi. Jump down and see what's happened."

Gidi, Snir and his driver were inspecting the damage. I stayed in the tank ready to fire in the direction of the town. I threw Gidi a flashlight. It was obviously going to take time to sort this out.

"Emmy, bypass me and set up a block towards Quneitra, at the next road junction."

"Okay. What's happened?"

"Crash. Pass us carefully. Tell your boys to go slow."

"Alright, we won't hit you," Emmy said confidently.

"When you reach the junction, deploy so you can see any movement on the road out of town, and get ready to fire fast."

Meanwhile, Gidi got Snir's driver to back off, and reported no special damage.

"Can't be," I said, removing my helmet.

"A tension wheel is damaged on Snir's tank. Our rear telephone torn off and the rear wall dented," he said hesitantly.

"I don't believe it. You stay here. I'm going down to look. Meanwhile, call up a technical crew to deal with Snir."

I checked the main drive wheels, worried that a hard blow on the axle would show the minute we began to move. Snir and his tank commander stood by anxiously. This was their first crash, but I'd been through it many times before.

"Okay, my friends, I'm going to try to move in the hope that everything's functioning. You get in touch with a technical crew and tell them exactly where you are. You're staying here alone, so don't sleep and be ready to fire at any time. If the fitters can't solve the problem, I'll send a tank in the morning to tow you."

I jumped aboard, and we began to move slowly as I anxiously watched and listened for anything amiss. But the drive wheel held. We seemed to be in good shape. I relaxed when we slid into position among Emmy's tanks facing the town. We could see the flashes of falling shells among the houses. Star shells kept Quneitra and the surrounding area in clear light, which helped us pick good positions. On the brigade radio, Yos was still demanding illumination to help him stop the Syrians coming down the Vale of Tears. Mizrahi answered.

"I haven't got any star shells. The ammunition is on its way to the battery. You'll have it soon. I'm doing all I can."

The officers in the brigade command APC seemed to be taking turns answering the radio, though Yanosh's voice was to be heard all night. From the radio traffic, I understood that the southern sector had been breached and that we had sustained heavy losses. All the reinforcements that were promised during the coming hours were being sent directly to the south. There was no indication of the size of our force that was committed.

Yos was travelling back and forth along the line in his APC. His positions were split in two: Zamir and Amnon on one sector under Yos' command, and Eitan on the other.

I could not see any Syrian movement in the direction of the town. A big building blocked our view of the explosions deeper inside. We were dozing from inactivity. I tried to stay awake, but the flesh was weaker than the spirit. I stood a while on the tank deck, but the cold drove me back inside. The men were asleep in their compartments, yet I knew one shout would wake them. Where were the Syrians getting their energy? We hadn't had a single hour to regroup and rest. Lack of sleep was bothering all of us. And it all seemed so desperate.

Yos—a lonely voice over the radio—continued to plead for illumination. What awaited us in the morning? Would I have to go back to the Vale of Tears to help Yos? Shells were still falling on Quneitra. I tried to guess the purpose of the bombardment, and my only conclusion was that they intended to take the town at dawn.

The Battalion on the move on the battlefield

Damaged Syrian tanks in the "Valley of Tears" beside anti-tank ditch

Brigadier-General Rafael (Raful) Eitan, Division Commander

Syrian mine clearing vehicle

Damaged Syrian armoured fighting vehicle (AFV) in the "Valley of Tears"

Kahalani and Battalion Staff Officers. *Right to left*-Dr. Alex (Doctor),
Lieutenant Ze'ev (Ordnance Officer), Kahalani, Lieutenant Gidi Peled
(Operations Officer), Second Lieutenant "Cobi" (Signals Officer)

Syrian BTR armoured personnel carrier inside Muzrat Beit Ju'an

21

OCTOBER 9, 1973   MORNING

The last hour of darkness was strangely quiet. Quneitra was quiet, for all the flames engulfing the buildings. Yos' sector was also quiet. By the first rays of dawn, I studied the ground ahead. There was no movement in the town. It seemed that the Syrians must have laid down the barrage on the assumption that large forces were stationed there.

The tank offensive against Yos began at dawn. Small enemy forces began to move forward. Yos and Eitan opened fire.

"Kahalani, Yanosh here."

"Good morning, Kahalani here."

"Move immediately into my area and hold ready as my reserve."

"I'm on my way."

Yanosh's command post was on a hill west of the crossing of the Quneitra—Mas'ade and Waset Junction roads—at a place we called Yakir-Kirton. Baruchin, assistant brigade operations officer, was there with three tanks as protection for brigade headquarters. We deployed to the east of them.

"Kahalani, you will serve as second line where you are."

I didn't understand what Yanosh meant by "second line." Was he expecting me to fight Syrians from these positions? Were we going to allow them to advance this far? Through the blinding beams of the rising sun, I could make out the shapes of some of Yos' tanks. He was reporting hits on enemy tanks, but with the sun in his eyes, he couldn't really judge the force that was coming at him. Next to me was Emmy's company with seven tanks and Major Yona's tank.

"Battalion commander, may we open battle rations?" my hungry crew asked.

"Are you crazy? We may have to move at any minute. Stay in firing positions," I said with a smile.

My crew knew me well enough by now, so the answer wasn't long in coming.

"We don't want to fight on an empty stomach."

"We'll find time for it."

I felt tense and uneasy with Yanosh's instructions to stay here. I knew I should be up there next to Yos—who must have taken heavy losses during the night. Ratess was deployed between Hermonit and Bukata, but all eyes were on the Vale of Tears. I scanned the terrain for a quick route across the road and up to the ridge, knowing that sooner or later Yanosh would have to send us there. He couldn't hold me in reserve for long.

Four helicopters—quickly followed by four more—clattered over Yos and down towards us. Yos' boys and mine scanned the fuselages looking for the familiar blue Star of David.

"Brigade commander, Yos here. Syrian helicopters overhead...."

The air was full of machine-gun bullets, but it was useless. The choppers looked like our French-made Super-Frelons.

"Is there a shell in the breech?" I yelled at my crew.

"HEAT round!" Gidi said.

For years I'd been thinking about hitting a plane with a tank shell. Aircraft attacking tanks always came in at the same precise angle and in a straight line till they dropped their bombs.

"Fire a shell at one of them!"

"A shell?"

Kilyon was astonished.

"Yes! Quick!"

The barrel elevated as the helicopters came on towards us. We fired and waited for the aircraft to disintegrate—but nothing happened. Later I heard that one of the helicopters was hit by a tank over Yos' positions and crashed into the Vale of Tears. From the discussions over the radio, that hit had an incredible number of fathers. Meanwhile, the remaining seven roared overhead. We saw our machine-gun bullets ripping into them, but nothing happened. Behind us they split into two groups, one continuing west over Kibbutz Meron Golan and the other turning towards Waset Junction. They were landing, no doubt with teams of bazooka-armed infantry. There was no one we could send. Now we were in a trap: Syrian tanks up front, and the helicopter-borne force astride our supply lines. Yos was already down to his last third of fuel and ammunition.

It was beyond my understanding how the Syrians could keep this up through four days and three nights. We had received no reserves, and I had no idea what was happening on the southern sector. Later I would hear that reservists were fighting there and pushing back the Syrians—who had reached as far as Nefah crossroads.

I didn't know how many tanks Yos had, though it couldn't be more than fifteen. I could hear them reporting shortages of ammunition. Yanosh allowed some of them to come down for refueling and arming, but he wouldn't let me move up. Nevertheless, I instructed Emmy to be ready for it, only to find that he had been listening in on the brigade frequency—a wise thing to do, though against standing orders. Yanosh finally came through when our nerves were almost at the breaking point.

"Kahalani, Yanosh here. Move out. Fast!"

We ploughed our way between basalt rocks and through thick weeds to the south road, travelling fast enough to throw clouds of dust into our eyes and nostrils. This time Yuval didn't disappoint me. He held on to the road surface. Emmy wasn't following yet. He would need a few minutes to organize before he could roll. Anyway, I didn't know what to expect on Yos' sector. The important thing now was to get there fast, even though we could see little through our own dust—and goggles would only make things worse. Once there, I would be able to guide Emmy to the best place.

"How many tanks have you got?" Yanosh asked. I didn't know what to answer. With my tank, we were seven, but the Syrians could probably hear every word we said.

"Prepare for substitution-talk report," I said, lowering my voice and resorting to a phrase that would send any monitors scurrying for their Hebrew dictionaries—if they managed to hear it all.

"Okay," Yanosh said.

"I am moving to Yos with forty," I said—then, making it sound natural, I added, "Correction. Another has just joined. I now have forty-one tanks."

"Fine," said Yanosh in a calm voice as he played the game. "I'm sending you three tanks that have just arrived, so you'll have a very big force. Good luck."

The conversation lowered the tension, though there was no reason why it should.

"Battalion commander, Emmy here. I'm on the road. Where do I come in?"

The distance between us was 500 yards.

"I'll tell you in a few minutes," I answered, then told my crew: "Be ready to fire."

We were now close to Yos' positions. His tanks were placed at random angles. Two tanks were moving back, apparently to refuel. But these weren't the positions overlooking the Vale of Tears. This was a ploughed field 300 yards farther back. I passed by a damaged tank and another that seemed abandoned, and moved into the northern sector towards the wadi through which the Syrians had come on the first night. A 15-foot high wall of stones crossed the field. We drove round it.

"Halt," I yelled at Yuval. He braked so fast that we were all jolted. Mere yards away were three Syrian tanks—two standing and one moving—obviously on the hunt for prey. I dived down into the turret and grabbed the handle to rotate the gun on to the nearest Syrian.

"Fire quickly!"

"What range?"

I thought I would go nuts. We were close enough that we couldn't miss, and Kilyon was bothering about range. All he could see through his rangefinder was an area of green—and it never dawned on him that all he was seeing was one Syrian tank at point-blank range.

"It's unimportant! Fire!"

The tank rocked as the shell left. Gideon rammed in another. I peered out. The Syrian wasn't burning, but I saw the commander leap clear and understood that he was out of it. I swung the turret round to the second enemy.

"See him?"

"Yes!"

This time Kilyon was enthusiastic.

"Then fire!"

Another shell went on its way. A hole opened up in the Syrian turret. I looked for the third—which had meanwhile stopped moving—and again traversed the turret. Beyond him I could see a fourth, coming quickly, its gun pointing straight at us, the barrel opening black and huge. A T-62!

"Fire! Fire!"

"Blockage," Kilyon responded apologetically.

The empty casing had wedged in the breech. Gideon heaved it clear as Gidi and I tried to help. I had visions of that menacing T-62 barrel and of death. My hands gripped the cupola rim, ready to heave me out if necessary. It wasn't. Accompanied by the usual noise and recoil, a shell headed in a beeline from us to the Syrian. As flames shot up from the T-62, I swung the turret again to face the fourth tank, which was rolling towards us. Kilyon scored a hit, but the Syrian kept coming—till a shell from another of our tanks somewhere in the neighborhood finished him off. I was covered in a cold sweat. It all seemed a nightmare. As the Syrian crews abandoned their tanks and raced for cover, I turned to find a good position from which to block the enemy advance.

I scanned the terrain, looking for the right location and watching for any other Syrians. With half an ear I was listening to the brigade and battalion radios. There were plenty of conversations with forces that I couldn't identify, but most of these were shut out of mind by some automatic selective hearing that only filtered through my own call sign.

Eitan came through on the brigade frequency to report that he was waging a fire fight to my right. Noting that I had come up to the line, he switched to battalion frequency and reverted to my command. Since he was already on the right flank, I turned east and deployed my tanks to hold the left. We couldn't see the Vale of Tears and were about 300 yards back from the ramps. While I was wondering how best to cross the open field to regain the ramp, a Syrian tank came up out of the wadi. I swung the turret and Kilyon fired. Two crewmen ran from the burning tank. Seconds later, another came up only to be hit by one of

my tanks. Controlling the wadi was going to need better firing
positions than these—but as I looked around for a tank that I
could easily move onto higher ground facing down the wadi, I
realized that I didn't know who was next in line to me and who
farther away. So I moved over to the opening myself.

From our new spot, commanding a full view of the gully as
it dropped to the valley, we hit five Syrians in as many minutes.

Around me were Centurions from a number of different units.
I didn't yet know that Yos, realizing the uselessness of remaining
in an APC to face tanks, had pulled back. Eitan was still under
pressure, but all in all, we were now placed to catch every Syrian
that came up over the ridge or through the wadi.

Whenever a Syrian fired, I found myself watching a strange
sight. No sooner did the gun shoot its projectile than the empty
casing shot out of an aperture in the side of the turret. I was
amazed at the speed of the loader/radioman. It was only later
that I discovered the trick: the T-62 was equipped with an automatic ejector. One thing was becoming clear. This newest ghost
in the Soviet-Syrian arsenal was as destroyable as the T-54 and
T-55 which preceded it.

"Kahalani, brigade here. Report your situation."

It was the voice of Shalom, brigade signals officer.

"We're on top of it for the moment. More Syrian tanks are
coming up and the artillery is slackening."

"Kahalani, brigade commander here. It's all your doing, believe me. My compliments to you and your deputy. How many
have been destroyed in your sector?"

"A rough estimate? Sixty or seventy. If you have any new
force that could take the forward line and consolidate the success
so far, we could destroy all of them. We can't let up for a moment
now."

I knew that if we could regain the ramps that we had lost
earlier in the day, victory would be ours. But the tanks of my
battalion were vulnerable and battered. A fresh force was needed
to regain the few hundred lost yards.

"Hold on. I'm waiting for reinforcements, then ... "

"Okay. You can relax for the moment. We're alright—and I
see that more vehicles are joining me."

"Kahalani, I'm making you responsible for the whole sector."

"There's a problem. Most of them aren't on my frequency. I can't communicate with the commanders."

"I'll get them over to you one by one. The only one who won't be with you is Ratess. I'll be pulling him back."

"Okay."

"Brigade commander, just a moment. Baruchin here. I have wounded that must be evacuated immediately."

"Bring them out—even if it has to be on a tank."

"On one of them, the tank commander and loader have been hit."

"Where are you?" I asked.

"I'm among the tanks. The damaged tank is forward. The line will have to move up if someone is to get near."

"Advance to the damaged vehicle and wave a flag. Others will move up to you."

I was worried. The brigade units were deployed in small groups, each on its own radio frequency. I even considered driving along the line to signal to each one the new frequency. But the Syrians were still coming, and I couldn't leave my spot over the wadi, even if only a few tanks could actually hear me. I had to wait for the brigade signals officer to do the job for me.

The traffic on the brigade frequency was heavy, and I barely paid attention to it. Then I heard Emmy calling me, but I was busy on the battalion radio and didn't answer. Yanosh came through and took a report from him on a large number of Syrian tanks coming up the wadi and the Hermonit. He sounded hoarse, excited and anything but clear. Yanosh asked him to pinpoint his position. Emmy replied that we were close to Hermonit, and that there were tanks behind us that didn't seem to know what to do. He asked Yanosh to assign them to us to block the Syrians.

"Ratess, Yanosh here."

"Ratess here," came the tired, weak answer.

"Are you to the right of Position Purple 426 [Hermonit]?"

"I'm in the area of 426."

"Spread out and move forward. There are enemy tanks to your front. The force to your left has reported them. Advance."

"Where to?"

"To the positions in front of you."

"I'm in the positions, and there are vehicles of ours in front of me."

"Move in among them."

"Alright."

The conversation astonished me. I couldn't see Ratess' tanks, though they weren't far behind. I tried to make contact with my neighbors but couldn't. Next to me was a burned out Centurion of ours, its skin ripped by exploding ammunition from inside. My own position was good, if dangerous. In the wadi, I could see scores of Syrian tanks moving confidently towards us. They obviously were determined to push us back, and it was just as obvious that we had to have our old positions on the ramps back if we were to stand. The others probably couldn't see what I saw. Turning my head around, I got a sudden glimpse of the sight Emmy had noticed. A line of tanks on the road behind me. I asked Yanosh who they were.

"Brigade Intelligence here," Ilan responded. "It's Ratess."

I relaxed at the sight of his eight tanks rolling in to reinforce us. I called Ratess, and he answered after a few seconds. This was my sector, and he had come to help me. Not only that, I needed him in the area where I was standing. But I was in a quandary. I had served in this man's tank crew when he was a company commander, and I suppose I was still in awe of him. Was I to order him or ask him? The last thing I could afford was to get his back up now. The stakes were too high.

"Are those yours on the road behind me?"

"I'm deploying to come in with you."

"Ratess. I would ask you to take the opening to my left and keep an eye on it. I'm going on to the ridges to the right."

That way I would be splitting the sector between us.

"Okay," he answered slowly.

I explained carefully where I meant, then waited for him to seal the gap. Syrians were still pouring into the wadi, but a little more hesitantly. Kilyon watched and waited for opportunities. Suddenly my attention was brought back to the brigade frequency. It was Baruchin.

"I have to pull back. Wounded man in my tank—and my other tank has a firing blockage."

The brigade operations officer asked him where he was.

"There are a lot of Syrian tanks where I am, ready to withdraw. I must get him out. I don't want anything to happen to him here."

I waited on edge for Haggai, the operations officer, to answer. Every tank was important now, and I doubted that the Syrians were about to withdraw.

"Evacuate them quickly to us," Haggai ordered. I wasn't too happy with that.

Shalom, the brigade signals officer, called to me.

"I'm trying to get all the tanks in the area on to your frequency. A unit has arrived with receivers of the old type, so we'll have to change your battalion wavelength."

"Hold on," I said, switching to the intercom and swinging the turret towards a tank that was trying to climb the ramps.

"Kilyon. Be prepared. Do you see him?"

"Where?"

"Behind the ramp."

"Yes."

The gun moved slightly as Kilyon made his last adjustment, then fired. The result was a cloud of dust.

"You were a little in front of him."

"Short. Correcting. Fire," he confirmed—and the Syrian burst into flame.

That was where we should be if we wanted to stop them occupying our positions. But it would take courage to get there. First of all, an advance in full view and head on to the enemy. Second, positions amid burning tanks—theirs and ours.

"Shalom, hold on a few moments," I told the brigade signaller.

Changing frequency now was a frightening prospect. Even a few seconds without contact might be catastrophic, especially since there were too many tanks not on the frequency now.

"All 'policeman' stations, battalion commander here. Start advancing to the ramps. We must hold them because there is a large enemy force beyond."

There were heads sticking out of cupolas down the line, as tank commanders looked around for a leader. I tried to identify the battalion crews, then noticed that the tanks which had come with Ratess were pulling back. I waved my arms frantically in an attempt to find out why, but the commanders ignored me. I called Ratess on the brigade frequency, but there was no answer. Ilan, the brigade intelligence officer, also took up the cry. Meanwhile, his tanks were still moving back and the Syrians were still coming on as if we didn't exist. I was helpless as far as Ratess' tanks were concerned, and would soon be for the whole sector. Without any ability to issue commands or check on implementation, the dense Syrian mass would bring us to breaking point. There was only one thing to do.

" 'Policeman' stations. Don't lose control over your neighbors. Move forward to the ramps. Now!"

"Amon here. Have two tanks with me. Am moving."

"Emmy here. I'm to your left. All my tanks are under control."

"Eitan here. On the right flank with two tanks from last night."

"Battalion commander here. If there are tanks next to you not on battalion frequency get them to switch now."

I hoped that hand signals would do it. I went on calling Ratess on the brigade frequency, and Shalom kept on talking to the incoming force, trying to direct them to us. I called him, but he didn't stop his conversation with the new boys. Finally I got through.

"Shalom, please get on to Ratess' frequency. He doesn't answer me. Try to talk directly to his tank commanders. Tell them that their effort must be at the wadi. The enemy is in there, and Ratess' tanks aren't in good positions."

Shalom promised to try.

Brigade Headquarters was to my rear. I knew that the staff officers knew my situation, but imagined that they couldn't conceive all the problems of the sector. It was up to me to restore self-confidence and get this motley group into one fighting frame by giving crisp and simple orders. I told Emmy to use flags to call the tanks around him up to the ramps. He straightened up in his turret and began to wave flags in both hands, but some of the tanks still took no notice. Finally he fired a machine-gun burst into the ground in front of one of them. The commander swung round and followed orders. Emmy continued to move slowly ahead, but when he saw that no one was following, he slid back into line. I was in a quandary.

Leave my position and slip to the ramps? Organize those who heard me and together rush to the ramps? Time was against us. I decided to try Ratess again, but Raful was talking to Yanosh on the brigade frequency. Something about a support force on the way to us, and the fact that Yanosh was already in touch with them.

"Ratess, Ratess, Kahalani here."

"Kahalani, Shalom here. Ratess took a direct hit. We have transferred all his force to your frequency."

A hot and cold current washed over me, ending in a cold sweat. I knew I was now the last battalion commander in the field. Ratess! Wounded? Dead? I prayed not.

"Shalom, Kahalani here, over."

I couldn't afford to lose him now.

" 'Egg' force has not yet contacted me," I reported, using Ratess' call sign. "Perhaps I should try their frequency?"

"I got them a moment ago and have transferred all that can be transferred to you. You'll have them in another minute."

Over the battalion frequency I tried again—and got the platoon sergeant of Ratess' Number Four Platoon, call sign "Constant," who told me that in his opinion they could all hear me now.

The sergeant joined Emmy's next attempt to head for the ramps, then volunteered to do the rounds of the tanks that weren't responding, to get them over to my command frequency. I liked his willingness and courage, and called him over to stand beside me.

"Sergeant, pay attention. Take over the spot where I'm standing and cover the wadi opening. Take care of any Syrian that tries to enter the wadi."

"Sergeant, Number Four Platoon here. Alright, but I'm out of ammunition."

That annoyed me. How do you take tanks into action without ammunition?

"Stay where you are, sergeant."

While I was thinking of another solution, I heard Zamir and Shalom on the brigade radio.

" 'Tiger' here," Zamir identified himself, "I'm on the right flank. . . ."

I tried to identify the tanks Zamir was reporting; they were from the large force that was moving towards us.

"Kahalani, brigade commander here," came the expected announcement.

" 'Tiger' here," Zamir pressed. "Request to move a little to right to take the controlling ridge."

He meant the Booster.

"Negative! Negative! Stay where you are! Kahalani, Yanosh here, announcement."

"Kahalani here."

"Pay attention. There's an attack on 'Tiger' on the right flank. Assist immediately."

"I want to climb the right ridge," Zamir said.

"Who is that?"

Yanosh waited for an answer, then continued.

" 'Tiger,' brigade commander here. Repeat—what's the problem?"

Still no answer.

"Kahalani here. Confirm. It's only a pity that the tanks that have joined me didn't make contact. I can't control them, and they're moving back all the time."

That point made, I started to look for Zamir.

" 'Tiger,' battalion commander here . . . "

" 'Tiger,' 'Tiger,' Kahalani is calling you," Yanosh joined in.

" 'Tiger,' 'Tiger,' battalion commander here . . . "

" 'Tiger,' commander here. An announcement."

Yanosh sounded hoarse and very tired.

" 'Tiger,' brigade here."

This time it was Shalom calling.

"Kahalani, brigade commander here," Yanosh said slowly, as though realizing the full import of his message. " 'Tiger' doesn't answer. He's under heavy pressure."

"Alright, I'll send one of my officers."

One more problem to add to a growing list. Shells were still raining down, hungry for targets. Amnon had lost his traversing mechanism and was now aiming by ordering his driver to turn the tank right and left. A shell hit the turret, but Amnon didn't feel it—until his loader/radioman flopped down inside the tank.

The shell, a hollow charge, had scored a direct hit on Avi Sandler. Amnon's gunner vomited. Amnon decided to evacuate the tank and crew. His small force now remained without an officer of company rank. Second Lieutenant Noah Timienker took over.

"Deputy battalion commander, Emmy's Number Three Platoon commander here." It was Ofer Tabori.

The voice was urgent, and platoon commanders didn't usually burst into the radio net—so I listened, even though my tank was firing.

"Deputy battalion commander here," Eitan replied.

"The battalion commander is dead!" Tabori yelled.

There was a sudden silence on the battalion radios. Eitan didn't acknowledge the message. I was too busy controlling our fire to do more than hear any reactions. Once our shells were away, I turned to the radio.

"This is the battalion commander. I'm alive. They don't kill me that quickly."

"Eitan here. That's a stone off my heart."

Tabori was in firing position when Major Yona was hit. Yona had stayed with Emmy in charge of a single vehicle even though I had promised him command over a force. He fought like a lion—till he was hit in the face. Ofer transferred to his own tank and headed to the rear while calling for Dr. Alex. The doctor met him halfway and transferred the wounded major into a personnel carrier, and Ofer returned to the line of fire. The medical team went to work on Yona's smashed jaw and breathing problems. Working under terrific pressure and tension, Alex performed a tracheotomy. Every second counted. Yona had stopped breathing. There were all the signs of advanced suffocation. The cut was made, the tube slid with difficulty into Yona's windpipe, and—to the relief of the team—the whistle of air reported that the operation was a success. All that remained now was to stitch the cut and evacuate the patient. Alex climbed to his feet with shaking hands, suddenly aware of the shells falling all around.

A tank ground to a halt next to the APC, and someone yelled, "The battalion commander's dead!" Agmon, one of our aidmen, leapt on board and peered down the turret. "He's not ours."

It was Ratess.

Yanosh was frantically looking for reinforcements for me. Eli Geva's company was refueling and rearming. Yanosh ordered Eli to move fast, but Eli reported that he hadn't finished refueling.

"That's unimportant! Go to Kahalani immediately!"

Yanosh was already talking to another force, sent up by Raful, though I couldn't identify who they were. Since Zamir wasn't answering, I ordered Emmy's force to shift to the right and reinforce Zamir's sector. I had decided to wait no longer. We must have those positions on the ramps.

"Sergeant 'Matmid' Four," I called.

"Sergeant Four here."

"I know your situation. Stay where you are and keep control of the wadi. Don't let one of them through. Clear?"

"Sergeant Four here. I remind you that there is no ... "

I slammed down hard on the communications override button. I didn't want the Syrians to hear that tanks of ours were without ammunition.

"I know. Stand high up where they can see you. That will keep them out."

I was ordering an impossible task, but I had no choice. The sergeant stayed where he was. I pulled out of line to the rear and swung to the right. As we moved, I looked over the area behind, searching for a suitable static line in case we needed to pull back in a hurry. I knew we mustn't give up the high ground and that withdrawal could turn into flight in seconds, and I was shaking at the very thought of seeking a rear line. I told myself that I wouldn't let it happen. If we lost the high ground, they could pick us off like flies. But then how could we keep on repelling them? That was a question to which I still had no answer.

" 'Policeman' stations, battalion commander here. All those who hear me—raise a pennant."

Of the ten tanks in my immediate neighborhood, most acknowledged my call.

"Alright. We must have those positions ahead of us. Otherwise ..."

A plane zoomed low overhead and dropped its bombs behind us. I shot down into the turret, then peered out as a second came over to drop its load. In astonishment I caught a glimpse of its wing markings. As if we didn't have enough troubles already. Switching to the brigade radio, I shouted, "Brigade commander, Kahalani here . . . Brigade commander . . . Our Air Force is attacking us."

"I read you," Yanosh acknowledged, then went on talking on the brigade frequency as if expecting division to hear. "Raful, Raful, Yanosh here. Raful, Yanosh here. The Air Force is attacking us. They must be stopped immediately. Over."

"Raful here. I'm stopping them."

Anonymous voices went to work on the radio. There were a few moments of despair, as I wondered how I could keep up with this situation, then . . .

" 'Policeman' stations. Battalion commander here. There's a large enemy force behind the ramps. We will move forward with the intent of occupying the positions to our front. Roll them."

I began to move slowly, looking around to see who was joining me. I waved at a few tanks, and they began to move, but agonizingly slowly. Suddenly two Syrians appeared on the ramps, seeking targets. We stopped and I grabbed the traversing controls and gave Kilyon a target. It was a terrible moment: we were completely exposed to the enemy and waiting for his shells, but the guns weren't pointing at us. Kilyon fired, as did others. I could understand my tank commanders. To reach those positions we had to cross open ground. From my previous spot above the wadi, I hadn't really appreciated how dangerous it was. Still, I was blessed with an excellent crew. Kilyon, for all his bulky build, was fast and capable of correcting his own fire. Gideon loaded at a blistering rate, while Gidi could almost read my thoughts before they were spoken. Yuval, who had improved considerably, handled the tank as if he were driving a small car.

"Battalion commander, 'Tiger' here."

It was a relief to hear Zamir. But the brigade communications officer beat me to it.

"At last!"

"I have three tanks in position, but I'm almost out of ammunition," Zamir said in tones of desperation.

"We'll relieve you soon," the brigade officer said. "Another quarter of an hour."

"I don't know whether we'll hold fifteen minutes."

"All brigade stations," Deputy Brigade Commander Jackie broke in, "evacuation of wounded to ammunition depot. Repeat, evacuation to ammunition depot."

I had now halted the attempt to regain the forward positions. On the brigade frequency, I could hear Yanosh briefing the commander of the force that was to help me. Raful told Yanosh that a battalion-strength Syrian force was grouping on "American" axis to advance in our direction, then asked whether Yanosh knew anything about Syrian tanks on Hermonit. The brigade commander didn't believe it. That was all I needed—enemy tanks firing down on us. Yanosh replied that he didn't know, nor did he believe it.

"Kahalani, Yanosh here. Report situation."

"Air Force attacked me—that you know. I want to advance, but have a serious problem with crews that aren't on my frequency. I want to move them forward, but can't control them. I've tried flags, but they advance then retire."

"I'm putting in the brigade commander of 'Toffee' on your flank."

Yanosh coughed, then continued.

"Do you understand?"

The brigade commander on "Toffee" frequency, at least before the war, had been Ben-Shoham. I didn't understand what he could be doing here when there were problems on the southern sector. Was it possible that he had been attached to our brigade?

"Please repeat."

"I'm putting the brigade commander of 'Toffee' in on 'Kirton' axis. Is that clear?" Kirton was on the way from Merom Golan to Booster Ridge.

But the voice answering as "Toffee" wasn't Ben-Shoham. Never mind. I would work the details out later.

"Morning physical training," Yanosh said—I didn't have the faintest idea what he meant. Besides, I had my own problems.

The brigade frequency was full of orders and reports to and from Yanosh. Zamir said he couldn't hold on; tanks were approaching from the eastern slopes of the Booster. Yanosh, worried, asked for a report. I didn't understand what "Tiger" was afraid of. After all, he was a part of my force—and I felt that we could hold. Perhaps he was under pressure from tanks that I couldn't see—or fire at? Unclear as it might be, I had faith in Zamir. He was a good officer. Yanosh prodded the "Toffee" brigade commander to move into position facing the Vale of Tears, on the right flank. Zamir was still radioing to brigade about the oncoming force, though with no details of range. He was beginning to annoy me. The brigade commander had more important things to do. Still, the presence of a new force was some encouragement. I knew that, with him, we would push the enemy back.

"Kahalani, brigade commander here. Have you got colored smoke?"

"Affirmative."

"Be ready to use for Air Force."

That was better. I thought of making a fresh attempt to reach the ramps, but the radio traffic was too heavy to allow me to concentrate on it right now.

"Kahalani. Air Force coming in within thirty seconds. Where do you think the biggest concentration is?"

Yanosh was going to try and direct them. From where I was, a mere 300 yards from the Vale of Tears, I couldn't see down. I could remember the lay of the land, and it was hardly likely that the Syrians could put any sizable force up the slopes to the ramps.

"Kahalani here. I'm not in position right now. They're coming up three or four at a time—and getting theirs as they reach the top line." I emphasized the Syrian vulnerability, though I knew I wasn't answering Yanosh's question.

"What's their strength?"

"Can't say ... Fire at him! Fire!"

The last was to Kilyon. His round struck straight and true, and I saw the Syrian crew jump out and run.

"Kahalani here. I repeat, I can't say how strong they are, since I'm on flat ground too far back from the slope—but we are waiting for them as they come up."

"Understood. I'm checking the possibility of sending you an organized unit. Hold on ... Geva, Geva, brigade commander here, over.... Geva, brigade commander here."

"Geva here."

"Are you ready?"

"Beginning to move. Am holding a moment to get them all on my frequency."

"Get them on Kahalani's frequency! I repeat—Kahalani's frequency."

"I read you."

"Brigade commander, Baruchin here."

"Go ahead."

"I'm next to 'Tiger.' Need reinforcement here, urgently!"

"I'm reinforcing with 'Toffee,' " Yanosh assured him.

The news that Geva was coming up with a company, and that reinforcement from "Toffee" was already in the area, encouraged all of us. Just a little longer to hold on till the new force arrived. I was scared that we would run out of ammunition, and I didn't know how many shells Eitan and Emmy had left.

"Brigade commander, 'Tiger' here," Zamir announced in an ominous voice.

"Brigade commander here."

"Red line. Can't hold any longer. Enemy pressing hard from the Vale of Tears. One of mine destroyed, and I must evacuate in tow."

"Okay. Do you identify relief force coming towards you?" Yanosh asked.

"Affirmative. Warn him not to fire at us. We've got no ammunition."

"The brigade commander of 'Toffee' is calling you on my frequency. Guide him into position."

Zamir talked to "Toffee," but they didn't understand each other. The newcomer, not wanting to approach the positions the wrong way, began to lose his temper. Zamir, obviously drawing on the last of his strength, didn't respond to the angry comments but continued to describe the enemy location. Yair, who was down near Position Seven on "America" axis and could see the enemy entering the valley, broke into the conversation and gave directions to the incoming commander.

Geva, on his way to me, made contact and came under my command. Seeing the dust of his tanks not far behind us, I decided that this was the turning point; now we must head for the forward line on the ramps.

Worried that they wouldn't all hear me, I looked for a new way to attract the attention of all the tanks. The Syrians could come up—and we were unable to hit them. Withdrawal was unthinkable, as was the idea that I couldn't get our tanks up to the prepared positions on the ramps.

" 'Policeman' stations, battalion commander speaking. Just look at the Syrians' courage as they come up to the positions facing us. I don't understand what's happening to us. After all, we are stronger than they. Now, start to move forward and straighten the line on me. I'm waving a pennant. Move!"

I had spoken quietly except for the last word. It was as if a spring had suddenly uncoiled. They were moving, some fast, some slowly—but they were moving! Yuval pressed down on the accelerator, and I found myself up ahead of the line. We slowed down to let them roll into place alongside.

"Don't stop! Don't stop! Keep moving! Keep moving!"

A Syrian came up to my right. I ordered Yuval to stop. Before I could swing the turret, a tank next to mine had taken care of the problem. I felt wonderful. The whole line was at long last moving towards the ramps. Now I was praying that we get there. With that line, we would win. Nobody would move us from there. They rolled, slowly and hesitantly, but not one of them stopped. Fifty more yards to go—and we would have the high ground, from which we could destroy everything that moved in the Vale of Tears.

"You're doing nicely. Don't stop. Keep moving. Be ready to fire."

Hands raised in turrets acknowledged my message. All I could see were the heads of tank commanders. They were scared. We were all scared—but there was no other way. Slowly I edged up into a commanding position and looked down into the valley. To my left was a burned-out Centurion—there since morning. Not far off were some Syrians that had reached the ramp only to be hit. Down below, the tanks we hit on Sunday were still in their places, and scores of others were moving through them towards us. The ranges were short—very short. Some of them were only yards from the ramps, and—given a few seconds more—would be on top. I guided Kilyon in on one of them, and he squeezed the trigger. All around, our tanks were firing like

animals bearing in on their prey. Behind us, guns were also
firing, and for a moment I was scared that we would be hit by
one of our own. The hail of our shells restored confidence. Each
tank commander chose a position, moved into it and began to
pick off Syrians. It was as if the gunners were settling all the
scores since midday on the Day of Atonement. Syrian vehicles
were burning, their crews scuttling back out of the field of fire.
We paid no attention to them. The tanks were more important.
Few Syrian guns answered us. Taken completely by surprise,
the Syrian armor raced for shelter—and there was none. We
knew we had won. We had the high ground once more, and
they were burning in the valley. I was still tense, worried that
some of them might have found breaks and got through us.
Geva came up and gave a strong arm.

Yanosh was in the middle of a conversation with Raful.

"Still holding the ridge, but the pressure is heavy, very heavy."

"Which axis is heavy?" Raful wanted to know.

" 'Kirton' and 'Kasserine,' " said Yanosh, referring to two
roads through the Vale of Tears.

"Is 'Morning PT' with you and in contact with the enemy?"

"Affirmative."

"Good. Good. They'll break eventually. Keep the battle thrifty."

"It's all very close range," said Yanosh.

"We're better than them. We're better than they."

"I know that. I tell you that we're under pressure all the time
and it's okay. No problems. I only need planes for the valley."

Down below, the number of Syrian tanks on the move was
declining fast. I could see "Toffee" force on the north slopes of
Bustar. Their commander was reporting his hits with great en-
thusiasm. The voice was familiar, but I couldn't place him.

Heavy artillery fire began to fall on our positions. There was
nothing to do but to duck down inside the turrets, even though
we lost efficiency that way. The first salvo dropped straight in
among our tanks. These guns had obviously been zeroed in
on the sector before. I contacted Yanosh and asked him to try
to silence the gunfire. It took some minutes till the guns were
silent.

The valley was a mass of "bonfires." The Air Force completed
its job of destroying the crossings over the anti-tank ditch. I told

my crews to look below for any Syrian tanks that might still be moving. But the task wasn't easy. Many scores of them stood immobilized. I estimated, together with the collection from Sunday morning, some 250 damaged or destroyed Syrians.

22

OCTOBER 9, 1973   AFTERNOON

Another tank had arrived at the battalion medical station. Off
of it came Second Lieutenant Avi Yahav, Emmy's Number Two
Platoon Commander. He had a head wound—not a serious one—
but he had lost his orientation. The doctor treated him, with the
shrapnel splinters still jutting from his forehead, and tried to
reassure him that his life was not in danger and that he must
wait for evacuation. Major Yona was still lying there. The helicopter hadn't arrived yet. Finally there was no choice, and the
two of them were loaded on a command car for the trip to Safad
Hospital. Sergeant-Major Moshe Zand, of "Zechar" Company,
who took the command car, kept insisting on a whirlybird and
finally got one. It put down in the fields of Kibbutz Gadot,
guided to a landing by a beacon of hay that Zand set alight.

Through the last three days, the doctor had been handling a
steady stream of wounded—and dead. Perhaps a thousand yards
west of us was the crossroads where the tanks brought their
grisly burdens. When they couldn't come to the doctor, he and
his team went to them.

Brigade Headquarters now focused its attention northward
towards the area around Bukata village. Suddenly a strange
voice broke through.

"Anyone who can hear me, this is Gur Two of Ampa
Company."

"Ampa, you are on a brigade frequency," said Shalom, anx-
ious as always to prevent unnecessary radio traffic.

But the nervous tank commander continued apologetically.

"Listen a moment. Perhaps you can pass it on. On the road
to the southern village—there's a gasoline station—on the
Quneitra-Waset—no, sorry, Quneitra-Mas'ade road. The Syri-

ans have invaded—infantrymen. Can something be done about it?"

The message was garbled, but that was understandable. The soldier who was reporting wasn't used to using a command radio net.

"Who's reporting?" Yanosh wanted to know.

"We're a damaged tank of 'Ampa.' Force 82. We're stuck here on the road up to Mas'ade."

"Alright."

"They broke through. About a company of infantry. They...."

"Okay. It's clear ... 'Ankor,' 'Ankor,' brigade commander here."

"Brigade commander, 'Ankor' here," Lieutenant Uri Kar-Shani, commander of the reconnaisance company, replied.

Yanosh ordered him to break off rearming and move north fast with all his vehicles—up to the entrance to Buk'ata. He told Uri about the tank and its report.

"Move! Destroy! Over and out."

Yanosh also sent into the area a Golani infantry unit that was posted to the brigade.

Artillery fire resumed pounding our positions with ever-growing intensity. When a tank to my left was hit, I finally lost my temper.

"Brigade commander, Kahalani here."

"Go ahead."

"The bombardment is continuing. Help me. They must be put out of action by our guns and air."

I had never before used the words *help me*—but now they expressed exactly what I felt.

"I'll do everything I can to help you succeed. You're a hero of Israel."

The blood flowed to my cheeks and I choked, unable to answer. Finally I managed to cough out a few words.

"The enemy is responsible for that.... At the moment, we're straightening the line and he's running. The problem is to trap them together in the passes.

"Don't take too many risks." Yanosh was also choked up, like a father talking to son. He repeated, "Don't take too many risks."

"I don't want you to stand down below while they hit us from above. You stick to tactical routes and good positions—not geography!"

"At the moment I'm holding the controlling line."

"Fine. I'll get some artillery on the ditch and the track alongside it."

"That's just what I need."

"Do you need more forces?" Yanosh asked.

"Not right now."

"To your right, our friend is working nicely." I was referring to the mysterious "Toffee."

"And he's welcome. It's okay. Now we're in control of the terrain."

"Be careful not to race too far forward. You might run into a rear ambush. Brigade commander 'Toffee,' do you read that?"

"If I haven't been hit so far, I won't be," I interrupted.

As Yanosh issued the necessary instructions to the artillerymen, I listened to reports on the situation of each tank and crew. Though I would have to pull back soon for fuel and ammunition, I felt absolutely wonderful; we had stopped a far superior Syrian force.

The brigade radio was now busy with reports on the battle against Syrian infantry to the north of us, in the area of Buk'ata, two miles distant. While that was going on, the commander of "Toffee" force was wounded; a shell splinter next to his. As he explained that the wound wasn't serious, I finally grasped the meaning of "Morning Exercises"; "Toffee" was my old friend Yossi Ben-Hanan—his father broadcast morning calisthenics every day over Israel Radio.

Yossi was married a month before the war—in a wedding that attracted all the top brass, including Defense Minister Dayan—and had come back to the war from his honeymoon in the Far East. He had been sent north and had organized a force of crews from damaged tanks with the help of Captain Shmuel Askarov, who had, up till a few months before, been his deputy. Shmuel was wounded on the first day but fled from the hospital to help organize the improvised force. Minutes before Yossi was injured, Shmuel was hit in the head by a bullet and again evacuated to the hospital—this time in a grave condition. But what was Yossi doing as brigade commander? What had happened to Ben-Shoham? I would only find out the answers in the afternoon, when Yossi and I would meet.

Since the job on my sector was done, at least for the time being, I slid down into the tank and perched on the commander's seat. Gidi was scanning the area through a telescope. Tired as I was, I listened to the brigade radio and could picture the drama going on to the north. It didn't worry me particularly because it was only one company of Syrian infantry.

Uri, the brigade's reconnaisance company commander, drove towards Buk'ata and established contact with the damaged tank that had guided him in to the enemy. Raful was interrupting constantly with instructions to other units of his command to move into the area where the Syrian infantry were reported. I couldn't identify all the troops engaged at Buk'ata. Uri sounded enthusiastic as he reported having made contact with the enemy. Yanosh warned him to check that they were indeed Syrians— and not our own paratroops. Uri replied excitedly that they were Syrian infantry, and he was taking care of them. The commander of Uri's Number Two Platoon, who was with Yanosh, reported over the radio hearing that one of the company's tanks had been hit, and asked permission to go for the wounded. He was asked to wait while Yanosh contacted Uri. The company commander confirmed elimination of the Syrian infantry, noted that a tank had indeed been damaged and that he was evacuating the crew to the rear. Yanosh again reminded him not to move too far to the east and congratulated him on the mission.

Minutes later Uri reported that he was grouping ready to move back. Yanosh asked him to come by way of the fuel depot and pick up the soldier from the damaged tank who had originally reported the enemy infantry.

"Brigade commander, this is the damaged tank. A force of 'Ankor' is in the area under fire from heavy ammunition from the north." The message came from Buk'ata.

Shalom, the brigade communications officer, asked Uri, "Are you under heavy artillery fire?"

"Very heavy!"

"Tanks or artillery?" Yanosh wanted to know.

"Artillery. My vehicles were damaged by the enemy infantry. Where's the damaged tank?"

"Are you engaged in rescue and evacuation?" Yanosh asked.

"Yes. I'm clearing out all the infantry," Uri replied.

"Good . . . I'm sending a force up to join you. Make contact. It's coded 'Tsaltzal.' "

"Listen, I have no problem. I have picked up the last of the men and am pulling out."

"Pass by the damaged tank in Buk'ata and bring that soldier in."

"Is the damaged tank the same type as ours?" Uri referred to Centurions.

"The same as your neighbor's," said Yanosh, referring to Haim's battalion. Haim had Centurions.

"I have taken out all the crews that were there."

"There's one more crew on the access route to the forward position."

"I don't think I left any there. I picked up the lot, including the infantry."

Haggai, brigade operations officer, was trying to make contact with the damaged tank. Uri insisted that he had collected the tank's crew, but Haggai ordered him to wait while he checked. Raful cut in to ask Yanosh to a meeting at Yakir-Kirton. The exchange with Uri was over, and after Yanosh left, a scared voice shouted, "Platoon Commander Ankor Three here. Bazookas from Mas'ade, from the east."

Raful's operators asked whether Yanosh was already at the crossroads, and received confirmation. Then Uri reported to Shalom, communications officer at Brigade Headquarters.

"I have evacuated everyone who was in the area. I am now with one of my units. Looks like there's a bazooka team on 'black axis' to Buk'atə. I'm going to deal with it."

"Good luck."

At that stage, I asked Brigade for permission to send tanks back to refuel. Yanosh asked me to wait a little longer. A few minutes later, an urgent call was heard on the brigade net.

" 'Ankor'! This is brigade operations officer. Get out of there immediately!" Haggai shouted a few minutes later. He feared a bazooka ambush.

"Okay. Getting out . . . But there's . . ."

The voice was cut.

"One, help him! Attack the Arabs so he can get out. Over."
Haggai was now shouting impatiently, but no one answered.

"Ankor stations, this is Brigade Operations. Get out! Get out
and give fire to assist evacuation of wounded."

"Brigade commander, Ankor Three here. Have you heard that
'Ankor' is hit at El-Rom?"

There was a sudden babble of voices on the frequency.

"Silence on this frequency," shouted Ankor Three. "Our APCs
were hit at el-Rom crossroads."

"Okay. Calm down . . . 'Tzaltzal,' this is Brigade Operations
. . . 'Tzaltzal,' this is Brigade Operations. 'Tzaltzal'! 'Tzaltzal'!"

Haggai's roars silenced all other traffic as we listened tensely.
Getting no answer, Haggai tried to raise the force on Hermonit,
to get them down to the crossroads and assist the evacuation of
wounded. It took a long time to make contact, but finally the
force reached the wounded. The operations officer of a Golani
infantry team got through to "Tzaltzal" force and sent them in
the same direction. The three brigade doctors were moved up
to Yakir-Kirton crossroads, where the wounded were brought.
They were treated quickly. Over the radio, there were still ap-
peals for help now and again from an APC that was still in the
field. I felt helpless at being unable to leave my firing positions
to do whatever I could.

Later we learned that the force identified by Uri had been
much bigger than a single bazooka team. The Syrians were con-
cealed behind rocks and in shrubbery. Uri took a number of
APCs into the attack with him, but they were greeted by a heavy
salvo of bazookas that put most of the vehicles out of action.
The battle was fierce and at very close range. Uri's force continued to use their machine guns and light arms, but the Syrian
fire was deadly. At roughly 1400 hours, the reconnaissance company for all intents and purposes was no longer effective. History
was repeating itself. In the Six-Day War, the company under
Uri's command had led the brigade into Rafia and had been very
hard hit.

I continued to sit inside the tank, my head resting on the
cupola, listening to the radio. We were exhausted, it was hot,
and eyes were closing. My crew made use of the lull to prepare
a midday meal. A little later, Yanosh radioed to repeat to us

what Raful had told him—we had that morning saved Israel. It sounded exaggerated to me, and I thought it was designed as a pep talk for the next moves. Still, Yanosh asked me to pass the message on to all my men.

I was given permission to send a few tanks back to refuel and rearm. Setting an order of priorities for this operation, I asked Eitan to go back and oversee it. The first tanks to go towed with them damaged comrades, both to evacuate the wounded and to enable restoration of the vehicles. I still didn't know who was among the dead and wounded, and I tried to thrust the thought aside for later. Of my battalion, I knew Eliav Sandler, a tank loader, had been killed, but all the force in the area was now under my command—and the names of the casualties were unknown to me.

The air was full of the smell of cordite and the smoke of burning tanks on the ridge. I felt an overwhelming urge to sleep—to forget it all. There were bodies beside the Syrian tanks; crewmen who hadn't managed to get away. In the wadi to my left was a damaged Centurion. I didn't know which force it belonged to, or how it got there. I wanted to check whether there were wounded in it, but the descent was too dangerous; there might be Syrians waiting to fire on a rescue mission. All of us wanted quiet, with no incidents that could revive the battle. But finally Eitan placed a number of tanks to give cover, then went down with Emmy. They reported that the tank commander was dead, and his crew was nowhere to be seen. I ordered them to evacuate the body as they were in any case pulling back to refuel. Farther down in the valley was the tank of Sergeant Zelig Haberman, with his body still inside, but it would have to wait.

When my turn came to refuel, I let Gidi guide the tank while I stood in the turret surveying the terrain. Ben-Hanan's tanks were drawn up in line on the Bustar, and his men were carrying out maintenance. The road on which we were travelling was pitted with shellholes, and its shoulders had been ground down by heavy tracks. On the ride back to the depot, I thought how proud I was of what our battalion had achieved. Gidi parked the tank alongside a truck of ammunition and the crew started to load shells. I climbed down, helmet in hand, to look for a quiet place to rest. I perched on a water culvert, then stiffened as I saw my brother Arnon running towards me.

As he asked, "How are you, Avi?" all eyes turned to the sight of two brothers embracing after days of combat.

"I'm fine. And you? I worried about you."

A tear rolled down my cheek, and I didn't brush it aside. I wasn't particularly proud of giving way to emotion.

"We've been listening to the radio. You were great.... We also heard what the brigade commander said to you.... Do you want something to eat, or drink?"

"No, thanks."

While we were talking, members of Arnon's technical team came up to greet me. They were all smiling, partners in the victory, their faces covered in stubble, their eyes bloodshot from lack of sleep, their hands grasping the tools of their trades.

"We heard you all the time," they said almost in chorus.

I smiled.

"What's this? Nobody shaves any longer in my battalion?"

We all laughed, then I turned aside as Captain Menahem, the brigade deputy intelligence officer, came over.

"Ben-Shoham and David Yisraeli are both dead." Yisraeli was Brigade Commander Ben-Shoham's deputy.

"What? Can't be ..."

"Yes, it's so. Sunday ..."

Now I understood why Ben-Hanan was answering to "Toffee" on the radio. A brigade commander and his deputy were usually low on the vulnerability list. But nonetheless, they got it.... Menahem didn't know how it happened but mentioned having heard something about them running out of ammunition while charging Syrian tanks.

"And what about the brigade?"

"I think it's been broken up completely. The Syrians got through as far as Nafah camp, and I don't know whether they've been driven back."

Menahem was rattling away as if I was ready to absorb all the lamentations of Job. Only now did I fully grasp the scope of the blow we had sustained—and just what this war was doing to us. While I was pondering that, Menahem announced, not without pride: "I hear that tomorrow we're breaking into Syria."

"Where?"

"Into Syria."

"Then they can do it alone," I blurted.

My battalion was in pieces. We had been blocking and par-
rying since Yom Kippur. My force was getting smaller and
smaller. Wasn't there any new force to do that job? Was it possible that all the burden had fallen on us? I wanted to shout it
out loud, but I didn't. I knew I mustn't say what I was feeling,
because somebody might take it as cowardice.

Later I met Yanosh and his staff officers. They were all exhausted. Yanosh said nothing about the men no longer with us.
The future was bothering him.

"We're to break into Syria," he said, trying to sound
encouraging.

"So I've heard."

"It's not yet clear when, but the men must be prepared for
it."

"What sector?"

"Do you remember 'Plan Gil'?"

He was referring to a scheme for a breakthrough near Forward
Positions Four and Five, in the area of Jubat el-Hashab, Tel
Dahur, Tel Ahmar and Taranjieh. Together we pored over a
map as Yanosh traced the routes through the line of mines.

I returned to our battalion position bothered by the question
of whether we were going to get hurt yet again. With me I carried
a map of the minefields, tank positions and communications
trenches along the frontier.

We spent the night where we were, the sector divided up
between Ben-Hanan and me. After dark I noticed that there was
an unprotected area between us. I explained to Ben-Hanan that
he must occupy it, but he obstinately insisted that it belonged
to me. We lost our tempers; finally I asked Haggai in Brigade
Operations to decide on the sectors for us. Till now I had been
responsible for the entire sector, but I didn't have enough tanks,
and we both wanted as many crews as possible to go back for
ammunition and a rest. To an onlooker, the argument between
us would have seemed ridiculous, but for me it was a matter of
principle. I thought my men were entitled to a rest no less than
were Ben-Hanan's, and I didn't let go until the sector was split
in two.

During the night, I called Amnon, Ami and Eitan to my tank
and explained to them what was due to happen. Once the mis-

sion was understood, even though I couldn't go into details, we remained sitting together to swap notes on the mad day we had been through. Amnon said he was glad to be back in the battalion after moving from command to command. Eitan remarked that the last two nights had been particularly bad, however—as usual—he was far more interested in getting out of me more details on the future. How far would we carry the breakthrough? Would there be additional forces? Emmy said that he didn't intend to restructure his platoons but would use two tank teams, with one firing and the other marking targets. He had used that technique the previous day and had succeeded in eliminating a great many enemy tanks. As far as he was concerned, seven tanks were an optimal number for a company. I agreed with much of what he said but postponed the rest of the discussion for the next day.

Though we had an easy night compared with its predecessors, I didn't sleep properly. The radio was broadcasting warnings of bazooka teams, and I gave permission to fire machine-gun bursts ahead and to the flanks every few minutes. Even though we couldn't know what we were firing at, anyone out there might reason that he had been spotted. Unfortunately, I didn't have any infantry or mechanized infantry to use as a deterrent.

23

OCTOBER 10, 1973

The morning was quiet. I looked over the ground and concluded that the Syrians weren't preparing another attack. At around 0800 hours, they sent over a few shells, possibly to remind us that they still had some strength. My radio went out of commission, and there were communications problems in others of the tanks. I called for Kobi, the battalion communications officer. He arrived in Amnon's jeep. As he descended, a Syrian soldier emerged from behind some rocks, where he appeared to have been hiding since the previous day. Gidi was furious—with me.

"See? I told you not to move far from the tank when you got down before. See how lucky you were?"

He was right. A few minutes before, I had walked through those very rocks. Meanwhile, Kobi kept his Uzi pointed at the Syrian who had become our prisoner. I dropped down from the tank to talk to the Syrian. It reminded me of one of those war movies where the prisoners were always brought to the commanding officer. This time it seemed different. I smiled. I couldn't whip up any feelings of hatred for the prisoner, who seemed no more than an unfortunate boy, unlucky not to have got away from us. I tried to talk by hand gestures, but he didn't answer. His only contribution to the conversation was an occasional "Bravo Moshe Dayan." I was angry with myself that I didn't know Arabic. At home we spoke only Hebrew, and when my parents, who were born in Yemen, wanted to keep any secrets from us children, they used a Yemenite dialect. Amnon's driver knew a few words. Finally we got out of the Syrian that he was a gunner in a T-62 that had been hit yesterday. He was dressed in a camouflage coat and volunteered that some of their crewmen wore coveralls, while others only had regular fatigue uniforms.

Kobi finished repairing the radios and took the prisoner—now relatively reassured—back with him.

Yos called through a few minutes later to tell me: "Your brother's here." I didn't understand. It didn't take Yos to tell me that Arnon was on the Golan, but he was actually referring to Yossi Melamed, my very good friend and his own deputy, who had been abroad—watching a basketball game in Barcelona. He had found space on a plane home and had come straight to Golan from the airport. I went over to meet him, and an emotional meeting it was, too. Yossi, in fact, was the first to hear how I really felt about the first few days of battle.

My tank crew was washing and changing clothes. I announced that I had no intention of following suit until the war was over. I badly needed a change of socks, but reckoned that if I believed the war would be over in a day or two, then I could hold out that long.

In the afternoon, Haggai, Yos, Ben-Hanan and I met at the entrance to El-Rom in order to take a look at the Syrian terrain. It was a very hearty meeting. Ben-Hanan and I even stopped by a staff photographer from *Bemachaneh*, the Army weekly, and asked him to record the moment for posterity. Next, Yos came over to me.

"You saved me when you arrived yesterday."

"Sure. Who fights nowadays with APCs against tanks?"

I tried to persuade him to spend the rest of the war inside a tank.

"I've been thinking about it, but I don't know how I'll manage."

"It's very simple. The radio links are the same as in an APC. They'll teach you how to traverse a turret, and you don't need to give the fire orders. You just point the gun at a target and estimate range."

I sensed that Yos had to change. We had gone through Armor School together and, as a mechanized infantry officer, he had learned to operate the Sherman. I didn't know what he remembered about the operation of a single tank. Yos didn't give a clear-cut reply, but he was seen later on a tank.

We went up Hermonit on an APC. The place had been hard hit by the barrage of recent days. The men, who had returned to the slopes the previous afternoon after being forced off earlier, relaxed. We went into a darkened bunker from which we could see the entire Vale of Tears. Every inch of it now seemed precious—after the blood it had cost. My tanks—looking tiny from three miles—were visible in their positions on the ridge above the valley. Below, in the valley, the scene was one of packed and smashed tanks, particularly at the entrance to the wadi and near the anti-tank ditch. From Hermonit we could see Jubata el-Hashab and the surrounding ridges. The area of breakthrough was visible, though the actual routes weren't. Ben-Hanan described it from his memories of before the war.

On the way down, we saw Katyushas being used by our men. It was the first time I had seen them on our side, and it was a wonderful sight. A truck stood close to the mountain, its tubes crammed full of rockets. The battery commander gave an order, and off they went, one after the other, making a sound like an air compressor suddenly releasing its load. Then I shuddered as I saw a burned APC, the brigade insignia barely visible, not far from the El-Rom road—a reminder of yesterday's reconnaissance company battle.

In the afternoon, we again went up to a vantage point, this time to Tel Varda. We took three APCs. Ilan—the intelligence officer—served as guide to the enemy deployment in the area. Yanosh pointed out the directions of entry into what would be our wedge. The briefing didn't really add much that was new. Yanosh also wanted us to bring our company commanders for the tour, but it was already late afternoon and there wasn't enough daylight left for it. What would happen in the Vale of Tears? Could we leave it unprotected while we moved into Syria? The question troubled me. Yanosh said that a tank platoon would be enough to seal the valley. I thought that it might serve as a deterrent but no more than that.

I decided to spend the night in the same positions; we felt secure in them, and we already knew the terrain. Yos and Ben-Hanan organized their battalions in parallel columns, each in a different area, ready for the following day. We agreed to call orders groups that evening. Returning to battalion, I told Eitan the essentials, then waited for a call from brigade. Time passed slowly until close to midnight, when I was called to Waset Junction for the orders group. I could have gone in a Jeep or APC, but I felt safer in my own tank. So we went—the whole crew. For the last stretch of road, we lit our white headlamps to avoid collision with any other vehicles coming towards us.

The junction is an important crossing on Golan. Now it was surrounded by tanks, APCs and Jeeps. Somewhere in the darkness, I spotted a tent "war-room" and edged the tank over to it. The area under the canvas, suspended from two APCs, was full of people. Thrusting aside the canvas doorway, I pushed through the crowd under dazzling light. The atmosphere was smoke-filled, and it was difficult to identify acquaintances, most of whom were in any case bent over to study maps.

Suddenly I spotted Lieutenant-Colonel Amos Katz. He hadn't been on the sector so far. I asked him what he was doing here, only to get a laconic "studying the ground." Amos had been on an advanced course at the U.S. Army Armor School. Leaving his family behind, he had returned home to put together a unit of men who had come back from abroad like himself.

Yanosh wasn't to be seen, but his staff officers were circulating and handing out background material. Maps were pinned up with overlays of the battle plan. I went over to the operations map to see where I fitted in. My battalion was scheduled as a spearhead on the northern route—the left-hand column. There were two main forces. The right prong was to be led by Ben-Hanan, followed by Yos. I was to be trailed by Amos. I was happy that we were once again the vanguard, yet a little concerned because the men were so tired.

Yair was also there. He wasn't taking part in the breakthrough, but Yanosh had assigned him to give cover to the vanguard forces. Aryeh, the artillery officer, looked worried; he seemed to be counting off the number of batteries at his disposal—and finding it inadequate. The battalion support officers were also there, Snir among them.

It almost seemed like a class reunion. The air was full of how-are-yous and what-have-you-been-up-tos. As the tension grew and the time of Yanosh's appearance approached, Haggai asked for silence, then called the battalion commanders up to the front row, where we would have a better view of the maps.

As Yanosh came in, we all snapped to attention. He waved us quickly back into our seats, then studied our faces, repeating the battalion commanders' names out loud by way of greeting, and perhaps to reassure himself that we were indeed there.

"Now the Syrians are broken. I'm telling you confirmed fact. It's important now to hit them hard and break them finally. Over the last few days, Ben-Shoham's brigade and our own brigade have fought some very hard containment battles. Despite the hundreds of tanks they used against us, we did stop them. Now they're worn down, there's nothing left but to go in after them. I want you to listen carefully, and try to stay alert. I know you are tired."

After we studied the battle map and the plan was clear to us, Ilan filled in the details of the enemy's dispositions and the topography of the area, paying special attention to the mine belts in front of our targets. I knew that this would be our main problem. Then he went on to discuss the ability to reinforce the line with tanks that were only thirty minutes behind us. He also noted the large number of enemy artillery batteries that would lay down a heavy barrage, and stressed that we could ease the fire on us only if they didn't identify us during the breakthrough phase.

After four days of combat, I wasn't particularly worried by the Syrian tanks. It was enough to locate them and to have them come out to meet us—and victory would be ours. Ilan didn't have exact figures, so we didn't know how many Syrian tanks had broken into our territory, nor how many were left on the front line. From the map that was handed me, the Syrian dispositions—in red, green and black markings—were dense, so much so that it was barely possible to trace the contours. The front line that we had to take consisted of a chain of hills with a web of tracks between them. To the south was the village of Jubata el-Hashab—where almost every movement was exposed to our eyes. Farther south was Tel Dahur, a hill easy to spot from miles away because of its distinctive light color and lack of foliage. East of Jubata was another village—Taranjieh—on the road northward; then, some kilometers farther on, also visible because of its red hue, the hill of Tel Amar.

Jubata and Taranjieh were on Ben-Hanan's and Yos' sector. I was to take Tel Amar, then continue along the axis of the road across a ridge that we knew as "Tank Ridge" to the village of Mazrat Beit Jan, while Amos would follow me on the mission.

Haggai spoke, after Ilan, about the deployment of the brigade. My battalion was given a tank-dozer, a flail tank against mines, a sapper platoon mounted on half-tracks, a mechanized infantry platoon on APCs and a battery of 155-millimeter guns to help us through the minefield. Our mission was to break through the forward line and the minefield, take Tel Amar, invest the positions around Mazrat Beit Jan, then take the village itself. Amos was to help with the breakthrough if necessary, then stand ready to take Mazrat Beit Jan. Haggai was brief and was mostly concerned with elaborating the tactical markings on the map. I asked when I would receive the support equipment and was told that everything would be waiting for me at the Yakir-Kirton crossroads in the morning.

Aryeh detailed the artillery support available to us during the breakthrough and immediately after it.

"The Air Force will begin bombing targets at 1100 hours, in other words, one hour before we are to break the fence. Judging by the number of sorties we have been allocated, they will not leave us much work to do. In addition, each lead battalion has a battery of 155 millimeter guns, and there are more batteries available to brigade. Their fire will be on target before and during breakthrough. Later, batteries will be assigned to battalions as required."

"Who will silence the enemy artillery?" came a question from the back of the tent.

"The Air Force and we have assigned some special guns to that."

"Who will be in contact with the air? Can we have them other than at the breakthrough stage?"

"I will be in constant touch with them," said Aryeh. "We might get air support later, but it depends on what they have to do on other sectors. There's another breakthrough to the south of us."

It seemed as if we were going to get strong air and artillery this time. Aryeh had already briefed the support echelons, and Snir caught my eye to confirm that he had all the details and would tell me later.

The usual procedure was for the brigade quartermaster to follow Aryeh with the logistic details of an operation, but Arthur wasn't there, so Ben-Shoham's quartermaster filled in for him with what we needed to know about fuel and ammunition. The supply trucks would follow the battalions to night laager.

Throughout the containment battle, Arthur Gafni had looked after our every need at the fueling depot. At one of my stops there, he told me proudly how hard it had been to get sufficient transport, but that the brigade lacked for nothing. We had fuel, ammunition, armorers and fitters. Each damaged or broken-down tank went straight to Sachs, the brigade armorer officer, and his men set to work immediately. When Yair Swet's tank was brought in, an electrician checking the firing mechanism touched a trigger. A shell that shouldn't have been in the breech winged straight into a fuel truck, which exploded, killing its two occupants. A chunk of metal from the exploding truck hit Arthur in the thigh. The brigade doctor and Alex began to treat him. Yet what seemed to be a small wound showed evidence of internal hemorrhage. Arthur was given a double transfusion and loaded on to an evacuation helicopter, but died on the way to the hospital. Neither Yanosh nor we would know that for a few days to come.

As the orders group proceeded, it was Shalom's turn to talk about communications. There were no major changes except for the new additions. Then he told us the location of Brigade Headquarters during the breakthrough.

When the staff officers were done, Yanosh got to his feet for the final briefing. He looked exhausted and his voice was hoarse. His towering frame left no space between the top of his head and the canvas roof. His growth of beard added years. He was wearing a coverall that appeared to be a few sizes too small, and clutching a small notebook in which he had recorded the main points of what he wanted to tell us. For the most part, he didn't refer to it.

"The most complex thing that I can see is the minefield which you see on the maps and which separates us from the targets. I want you to carry out that stage slowly and safely. You have tank-dozers, mine flails and sappers. All three will help. The minefield is marked, and you'll see it as soon as you cross the frontier. It's important that you mark your pathways clearly, because large forces will probably be following—and I don't want the route to vanish. I don't mind if you leave men to mark the paths throughout the day. While you're dealing with the minefields, you'll have heavy artillery on the targets, so the Syrians shouldn't be able to spot the breakthrough points. They will have difficulty in engaging you with their fire. Now, I assume that there will be heavy gunfire, both ours and theirs, so the dozers and flails will work under barrage."

He went on to explain once again how to go through the minefield, to emphasize how critical this stage was. And it worried me. I wasn't among those who trusted the equipment we were being given, especially not on basalt rock, with which I had no experience. Yanosh also had something to say about all the combat possibilities we might encounter.

"It may be that one wedge will afford passage for the entire brigade. I will coordinate between the battalions based on what I hear from you, so each of you must be prepared to take on missions that are not in your present assignment. Any changes will reach you over the brigade radio."

That meant that we each had to study the areas assigned to the others. I sketched in thin lines to show my breakthrough route and the stages of combat that it would entail. I didn't want to mark too much on the map, for fear that I wouldn't be able to identify the contour lines and landmarks, but I did sketch in very lightly Ben-Hanan's routes and stages.

"The moment we sit on Tel Ahmar and Taranjieh, the situation will be completely different because we'll be in control of the terrain."

While Yanosh spoke, I glanced round at Ben-Hanan. He was asleep, bent over the maps in his hands. I nudged him and he woke up, making as if he had only been studying the maps. Much as he tried, his eyes closed again, only this time Yanosh noticed it. He asked Ben-Hanan to sit up and try to stay awake. My eyes were also closing, but the tension helped keep me awake. After he had covered all our moves for the next day, Yanosh repeated that we would now smash the Syrians to complete their downfall on Golan.

"Remember those who are no longer with us. The whole nation is behind us in this operation, and we mustn't disappoint them."

He had finished. Now we were free to make our final checks

with the staff officers and to return to our battalions. Jackie, the deputy brigade commander, came over to tell me that the armorer had some repaired tanks at the crossroads, and I could have a few of them. I only had twenty tanks, and any addition might make a significant difference. He tried to sell the idea to the other battalion commanders, but they didn't seem interested; they were too deeply immersed in their preparations for the breakthrough.

It was 0200 hours, and I was wondering who I could send at such a late hour, but the opportunity was too good to miss, despite all my fatigue and the need to sleep till dawn. Finally I decided that it would be impossible to bring the tanks up during the night.

"Avi," Yos suddenly said, "what about the tank you promised me?"

Yos had received Geva's company less one tank that stayed with me, and had spent a whole day begging me, over the radio, for that tank and crew.

"Yos, I'll let you have them tonight, but I have a problem."

I knew he would help me out.

"Laor is with your battalion, as deputy company commander under Geva."

"Yes, he is with me."

"Alright. He slipped through my fingers. I have tanks for him, and I must have him back as company commander. I need him urgently."

"Avi, he's Geva's deputy, and if he goes to you, I'll be missing a tank and a deputy company commander."

"What's a deputy? I need him to command. I had him, and somehow Geva snatched him away when he left on Tuesday afternoon."

"Okay. I'll give him to you on condition that you return that tank of Geva's that stayed with you."

I agreed, then drove off to meet Laor and give him instructions personally. Yos' battalion was near Merom Golan, and I only found them with difficulty. In my tank, I drove slowly down the company lines, asking whoever was awake where I would find Laor. Finally we made it, and Gidi jumped down to call

Laor. He scrambled up onto the tank, half-awake and astonished that anyone would want him at this hour.

"Laor, there's a war tomorrow and you're sleepy? What's happening to you?"

"They're all asleep . . . and I finished preparations," he muttered drowsily.

"Tell me, you no longer want to fight with your own battalion? Found a new one, uh?"

"Well . . . Geva asked me, and . . ."

"Alright, I know. No need to apologize. Do you want to be a company commander in this war, or a deputy?"

"Come on, what sort of questions are you asking me?"

From his smile, I knew he was finally awake and absorbing what I said.

"Listen, Laor, I've fixed it with Yos. You're coming to me as company commander."

"Great!"

"I want you to go to Waset Junction. There are tanks and crews there. Take a few and come on to battalion."

"Whom do I ask for at the junction?"

"I don't know, but I think the brigade armorer is there organizing them."

"How many tanks are there?"

"Don't know, but I guess between five and ten. Laor, it's a special job for you. Get over there, pick yourself a company and come to battalion in the morning."

"Where do I meet you?"

"Right now we're in the firing positions, but stay in touch on the radio. We'll meet wherever we are in the morning. It's important that you tell the crews which battalion they're joining and what their mission is. Split them into platoons, and make sure they all know you. They must know with whom and for whom they're fighting."

"Sir, trust me. It'll be okay."

I sagged down into the tank, rested my head on the cupola and told Gidi to take us back to battalion.

"Kahalani, we've arrived," Gidi woke me.

I was surprised that he used my name. I made a habit of

insisting that the men not address their commanders by name. I believe in military discipline, and one way of getting it is by instilling reference to job rather than personal labels. Yet I understood Gidi. We had become very close over the last few days. It wasn't strange to be called by name rather than "battalion commander" coming from that proximity, yet it still grated even if I could understand the need to break down barriers in such conditions.

"Gidi, we'll have an orders group in the morning. Wake me at dawn."

Gidi arranged the sentries. In the two hours I still had to sleep, Laor called a few times to say that he couldn't locate the armorer and the tanks I mentioned. I called brigade to try to get the armorer or the deputy brigade commander—but without any luck. Finally Laor found them and started to organize the tanks to move into battle.

24

OCTOBER 11, 1973 MORNING

The engines were started up at dawn, and we stood ready for contact with the enemy. Then came a message from brigade to be prepared for a session with Yanosh at Waset Junction. I used the time to prepare my tank—and made sure that the rest of the battalion was doing the same thing. Laor was still at the crossroads. Eitan, Ami, Amnon and Snir came over to my tank where I gave them a quick rundown on our assignment. I thought of moving the tanks down to the road, then decided it would be best to stay put. I had already told Eitan and the company officers the night before that if I radioed from the brigade orders group I was sending four more tanks to the sector, it would mean that I wanted the lot moved down to the road.

I didn't have long to wait for the call to brigade, and again went down with the tank only to wait a while until Yanosh arrived directly from a consultation with Raful and the chief-of-staff, David Elazar.

"The chief-of-staff and the commanding general said that this operation will smash the Syrians completely. Data were presented to show that the Syrian Army is broken. This is our chance to force them to an armistice on our terms."

Yanosh's words were encouraging, but it still seemed an impossible mission with forces that needed rest and regrouping. He retraced the different tasks on the map, reminding us that we must report at certain critical points.

"We will move out at 11:00, when I give the word, and each of you is to confirm."

"How about a code word to start," Yos suggested.

"You're right. Who's got a word?"

He looked at us and waited. I was studying the map, not

particularly caring what was chosen—then I suddenly realized
they were all looking at me.

"Kahalani, you must have a good idea."

"What idea do you want from me? What difference does it
make?"

"Come on, 'Panther,' throw us something," Haggai smiled at
me.

" 'Black Panther,' that's it," Shalom and Ilan yelled in chorus.

Days before, when we were under heavy pressure, I received
a radio warning not to let Syrian tanks bypass me. I had jokingly
replied: "They wouldn't do that. They know they're dealing with
a panther." Haggai had promptly asked: "What panther would
that be? A black one?" I had forgotten all about it, but the others
apparently hadn't.

We brought our maps up to date with new information, hur-
rying now because there were only two hours left to zero hour.
I still hadn't spoken to the battalion. It was worrying me and
must have shown on my face.

"Kahalani, come with me for a moment."

Yanosh led me aside, his arm around my shoulders.

"Listen, I told the chief-of-staff what you did in the containment battle ..."

He broke off, obviously choking with emotion, just as I was
at that moment.

"I told him you were a national hero ... I wanted you to know
that ..."

Much as he tried, the lump in his throat would let him say
no more. We shook hands. Feeling the blood flushing my cheeks,
I walked back to my tank, leaving Yanosh standing there another
moment. I was feeling guilty; perhaps he had taken me aside
because he read the worry in my face. We parted like men who
might never meet again.

Back in the tank, I radioed the message that I was sending
four tanks. Eitan replied that all was well and he was waiting
for them. A few minutes later, I spoke to him again. I asked
whether he had received the tanks. From his question about the
direction they would come from, I gathered that he hadn't
understood our agreed code. There was nothing for it but to ask
Amnon to go over and explain to Eitan that I wanted the tanks

down on the road. So much for prepared code words! Anyway, by the time I got there, the battalion was drawn up in columns of companies on the Mas'ade-Quneitra road, and again there was a feeling of a big battalion; Laor had arrived with his newly co-opted company.

Eitan had all the officers gathered together at one spot. Technical crews were working their way down the lines repairing last-minute faults. Command cars were circulating, distributing clean underwear and socks. My crew collected theirs without forgetting me, even though I had sworn not to change my socks till the war was over. On my way to brief the tank commanders, I was intercepted by Gidi, my operations officer, who insisted that I remove my windbreaker. I couldn't understand, but he persisted: "I don't think it looks nice." I looked down at myself and had to agree; my coat reached almost to my knees, there were no rank badges, and the epaulets were torn. It was warm and comfortable—but I accepted Gidi's point.

I looked at the commanders and got a shock. I knew fewer than half of them. Some had come with Laor, others joined during the recent battles and were, at best, voices over the radio. Then there was the sapper platoon—consisting of reservists—the tank-dozer and mine-flail commanders and two APC officers transferred from Yos' battalion. Here we were about to embark on an invasion of Syria, and I still had to introduce myself to my command—tell them what their mission was and which unit they had joined.

"I see a lot of commanders whom I don't yet know," I opened, surveying the rows of men arranged by company, each with his personal weapons and all looking exhausted.

"Alright, for those of you who have only joined today and don't yet know where north is, it's behind you. You are in Number Seventy-seven Battalion of the Seventh Brigade, and its commander, Kahalani, is standing in front of you."

That raised a hesitant smile. Meeting a new commander is always an uncertain moment, and certainly so in these conditions.

"Before I explain our mission, I want to know who each of you is, and what your jobs are."

One by one, each told me his name, company and tank number. I asked each what he had done so far in the war, and about his unit. Men with Laor's seven tanks were drawn partly from Ben-Shoham's brigade and partly from reservists who had joined the war a little late. There were others who seemed to have arrived here without rhyme or reason. The two support tank commanders were from different units, and neither had any real training in the use of their tools. The two APCs had brought mechanized infantry who belonged to brigade, under the command of Lieutenant Lutsky. Once the introductions were completed, I could continue the briefing.

"Alright, friends, the battalion that you have joined has high performance standards. During the last few days, we have been in a tough war. I want you to acclimatize quickly. Get to know your commanders and your crews—and become an organic part of the battalion."

With Gidi helping to hold the map, and using a folding pointer that I always kept in my pocket, I traced the main points and routes.

"The brigade is to break the Syrian line, take Jubata, Taranjieh, Tel Dahur and Tel Amar, then stand prepared to take Mazrat Beit Jan. The column will move in the following order: after me—Emmy with H Company, Amnon with M Company and Laor with G Company. The dozer and the mine flail will move with Emmy's company as a part of it. Sapper platoon will be ahead of Laor and will advance when ordered. As we cross the frontier, the Air Force will be bombing the targets. As for the artillery, I want it to roll 200 yards ahead of the tanks, as a wall between us and the Syrians. Snir, I want scorched earth in front of us—and please don't save on ammunition. I don't want casualties. The war will soon be over, so you fire without any limitations, clear? As for the minefield, Emmy, you'll bring forward the flail tank and break through with it. If that doesn't work, then try the tank-dozer. After that, there is always the last possibility—the sapper platoon doing the job on foot."

I turned to the combat engineer lieutenant.

"Tell me, my friend, have you got detecting rods and marking tapes?"

"Yes ... and bangalores to blow the opening. You only have to tell me where and when."

He was a reservist, about thirty-five, with a bushy mustache and plenty of self-confidence—the kind that comes from know-ing the job.

"Okay. I hope we won't need you."

As I continued to run through the briefing, I had a feeling that I had done all this—almost word for word—somewhere before. Then I remembered: outside Khan Yunis in the Gaza Strip on June 5, 1967.

I pointed out that we would probably be moving along one axis, in a column, so our forward firepower would be limited to a few guns. After questions were answered, I concluded with a few points:

"If a tank gets hit, I don't want it neglected. Another tank—but only one—will offer assistance. If the crew doesn't need evacuation, then they will stay with their tank and defend them-selves until the rig can be moved. I want each tank to cover its comrades, even if it means close-range fire. Our route will com-pel us to move in column, so proper cover is critical. Any tank that gets stuck, for any reason, will report his position to a technical crew."

I checked that they all knew the frequencies of the technical team and of casualty evacuation.

"The doctor and armorer officer are to follow the column by not more than 200 yards. I repeat, 200; our tail is long enough already. I wish all of us luck, and I want to see you fight like lions. We have twenty minutes till we move out. Get aboard your tanks and be ready."

I kept the company commanders and Snir a minute more to check that the axis of advance was clearly marked on their maps. Then I asked Ze'ev, the armorer, where my brother was.

"Repairing tanks at the Waset Junction."

"Fine."

I wondered what I would have done had Arnon joined the technical team with the colunn. I guessed that Ze'ev probably had thought about that and had assigned Arnon accordingly.

Radio traffic was building up on the brigade frequency. Bat-talion commanders were confirming readiness for "Black Panther." At 11:00 I reported to Yanosh.

" 'Black Panther,' repeat 'Black Panther,' over."

"Received. Good luck."

We rolled on to the road and moved north. It was a long column, and we had about an hour to go to target. Since Mount Hermon was no longer in our hands, I was sure they could see our movement from up there. The shells would soon be falling. Our planes were passing low overhead, crossing the frontier and dropping their loads on our targets. There was anti-aircraft fire, and I could even see a few missile contrails passing the planes, but none seemed to be hit. Smoke mushrooms were billowing over Jubata el-Hashab and Tel Amar.

My worry now was dropped tracks as the tanks raced to keep station in the column. There were dangerous curves ahead, and I warned the company commanders about skidding. One tank askew on the road would stop the whole column before we even began. As we rolled past two burned-out APCs, I was reminded of the infantry battle at Buk'ata and of the fact that we were the first to use this road in the last twenty-four hours. There could still be Syrian infantry teams in the area, so I held my machine gun ready.

I felt just as I had in the Six-Day War; then I was a company commander in Ehud's battalion. He was in the right column with two tank companies (Benzi Carmeli's and Gilad's), and I was in the left, with the battalion's mechanized infantry company behind me. I led the column and was the first to cross the border in that war.

I looked back at the tank commanders. Most of them stood with their heads in the turrets, tensely expecting the Egyptians to open fire on us. The battalion commander and the tanks following him had a hard time finding the way into Khan Yunis, and I went on to cross the border. I felt the importance of the hour; I understood that we were starting the shooting war. So I got on the communications net: " 'Builder' stations, this is 'Builder.' Take note: the time is twelve minutes to nine, June 5, 1967—at this very moment we are crossing the border. We are making history. Good luck to all of us." When I finished, the tank commanders stood up in their turrets and signalled with a wave of flags that they had received my message.

The road into the village of Abasan el-Kabir led me onto an axis that was hemmed in on both sides by cactus bushes. Heavy machine-gun fire opened up on my tank, but I sensed it only

when I saw flakes of paint twitching on the turret; I didn't hear
the sound of the fire because of the earphones and the racket
being made by the tanks. I immediately dived into the turret
and ordered my gunner to fire left and right into the trees, even
though I couldn't make out the source of the fire.

Then the road became narrower than the width of a tank. I
couldn't move back because the whole company was moving
behind me in a column. To reverse would have been a complicated and time-consuming operation. I kept moving, trying to
break through the cactus bushes. Suddenly a tread of the tank
broke. I felt awful, getting stuck like that and holding up the
entire company. I asked for covering with machine-gun fire. The
tanks let loose a hail of bullets in all directions.

Nuri Conforti, the commander of Number One Platoon, who
was behind me, moved into the tank behind him. After telling
my crew to be ready to open fire if attacked, I jumped into Nuri's
tank. The commander of the tank that Nuri took over jumped
out and ran over to my tank.

I edged back a bit and managed to break through to a new
path that bypassed the one where my tank was stuck. The company column continued moving behind me as I took pains to
keep moving straight, fearing mines at the sides of the road.
After advancing some 1500 feet through the yards of the houses,
I was forced back onto the main road, where the tread of my
new tank broke.

I looked for another tank to get into. The last two in the column
tried to bypass those in front of them, moved off the road, and,
a few yards on, hit mines. My frustration was growing as I
thought that we were starting the war on the left foot. I wasn't
used to fighting in column formation, but that was how things
stood and I had to make my peace with it.

I saw that Zafoni, my second-in-command, was moving in
my direction. I raised him on the net, and he pulled up beside
me. After quickly briefing my second crew, I climbed into Zafoni's tank and kept going, breaking open a new axis, with the
whole company following. Later the road was blocked by a bar-
ricade of trees, stones and tin barrels, but one shell blew it all
to bits. A bit farther on, two children jumped in front of the
tank and ran like scared rabbits. I followed them down a road

that didn't allow them to turn right or left. I could see their mother standing in a bend, her hands raised as she screamed in terror. I wanted to tell her that I wouldn't harm her children, but there was no way I could do that. The two children continued running as my tank moved a few yards behind them. I waved to the woman when her children reached her arms; she embraced them, nodded a sign of thanks to me and disappeared.

We drove through the village and entered Khan Yunis, moving in column formation and firing incessantly at the infantry in the yards at the sides of the road. The system was to have the tanks move down the street quickly as they covered each other with machine-gun fire. The fire from the tank behind me whizzed right past my head as it sought out the infantry lying in the trenches alongside the road. Zafoni fired to the left with an Uzi while I fired to the right, with the aid of the 0.5, and from time to time we both hurled grenades into the trenches.

On the occasions when we didn't fire, the local Arabs didn't know which side we were on—some of them applauded and flashed victory signs as we came by, others ran in panic. Cars that had fled from Rafiah were beginning to reach Khan Yunis. Using flags, I signalled the drivers opposite me to clear the way. The scene resembled traffic in Israel on Independence Day: the road was filled with tanks moving one behind the other in an orderly and confident parade.

The cars and trucks on the road let us pass, and the soldiers inside them looked frightened. But then one of the trucks refused to move off the road. My driver was moving at a clip as the gunner searched for targets. There were about ten soldiers on the recalcitrant truck. In response to the driver's obstinacy, I pulled my whole body up through the turret and signalled him with a flag to get off the road. Suddenly I sensed that it was too late, dropped the flag, and moved to turn the cannon to the right. The gunner, without realizing it, kept peering through his sight at the truck, so that as we moved along, the cannon was turned to the left. I didn't have enough time to move it back—everything happened too quickly—so that the cannon crashed into the truck. In the impact, the cannon shaved off everything in its path. The truck's driver and the soldier sitting beside him were killed instantly. I didn't see what happened to the rest of the men in the vehicle because my turret swung back, dealing me a sharp blow to the back. The truck remained there in the middle of the road as the tanks behind me skirted it. Later I discovered that the cannon's firing mechanism was damaged by the collision, and I couldn't fire any shells.

25

OCTOBER 11, 1973   AFTERNOON

The Syrian village of Mas'ade seemed deserted. Windows and doors were closed. Occasionally someone peeked out, as if to see what was making all the racket in their village. Panic-stricken dogs were racing about, and cows milled around the yards. The descent through the village was dangerous, but passed without mishap. As we passed the volcano crater lake of Birkat Ram, I ordered Laor to wait in the parking lot of a nearby restaurant. I didn't want to arrive at the breakthrough point with the entire force. We climbed towards Forward Position Four, immediately above the frontier. The noon sun warmed our faces, and everything was calm—the quiet before the storm. On the way up, Emmy reported that the two support tanks were no longer with us. I would have to go through without their help. Three hundred yards from the frontier, I pulled over to the side of the road with Snir right behind me and waved Emmy to keep moving, then slid into a slot in Emmy's company column. Snir was still directing heavy gunfire on to our targets, but the Air Force, having completed its mission, was no longer to be seen.

Over brigade radio, I heard that Ben-Hanan was already in stage two. Shells started to fall around us. We ducked down in our turrets, while I tried to locate the source of fire. Obviously, the Syrian fire was being directed from Mount Hermon, and we would be visible to their artillery spotters all the way. We kept on moving, but the rain of artillery fire was gaining in strength. Some twenty Syrian tanks stood along the road—victims of our forward tanks, which had been protecting Positions Four and Five, and of Ratess' battalion, which had been to the north of Hermonit when they crossed in the first days.

Emmy pulled up on the road. To his left, I saw a gaping hole in the border fence; the gap through which the Syrians had come at us. The temptation was great; if we followed their tracks, we need not fear mines. But, on second thought, it would take us north of Tel Amar—our target—and would force us to seek alternative routes.

Time was pressing. I decided to cross in the area originally marked, though there was no clearly defined track, and left Emmy to find an answer to the problem once we were through. His tank crushed the fence. He had his hand on a machine gun, his eyes flicking left and right as he sought an easy road. Thick foliage next to the fence forced the tanks to maneuver among trees, but—apart from the shellfire—no one hindered our progress. The Syrian guns were remarkably accurate. Then it suddenly dawned on me that these shells somehow sounded different from the ones we had been hearing. I slammed down on my transmitter button.

"Snir, battalion commander here. Cease fire. Cease fire immediately!"

As if to emphasize my point, a large chunk of shrapnel hit Gidi's helmet and tore the rear part away. Gidi flopped down inside the tank, removed the helmet and stared at it in stunned surprise. We were trapped. The trees left us no room to maneuver clear of the shell-swept area.

"Snir! Snir!"

I had to be right. We were in Syrian territory now, and they wouldn't be firing at their own positions.

"Battalion commander, Snir here. I have stopped firing."

"Your guns are shooting at us," I yelled into the microphone, though I still wasn't absolutely certain about it.

"I don't know what happened. I'm checking."

Snir sounded ashamed of what his comrades were doing to us. Be that as it may, within minutes the area was quiet but for the roar of our engines. Through the trees, I could see Tel Amar, and the mound was now serving as my point of reference for navigation. Emmy was ploughing on through the foliage. Behind us Amnon was through the gap. Now I was ready to order Laor forward, since I didn't want too big a gap between us and a third of the battalion.

"Battalion commander, Emmy here. I've reached the minefield."

"Is it clearly marked?"

"There's a fence."

"Hold where you are."

The support tanks were stuck, but maybe they were out of it by now. I asked Emmy to check whether they could join him.

"I have. The mine flail might be able to, but it will take hours."

Bringing up the sappers on their half-tracks, through trees, seemed too complicated. I called the platoon commander and told him to move forward, just in case, but I couldn't afford to wait. There were signs that the ground where we were standing had been cultivated.

"Emmy. This ground has been cultivated. The fellahin must have had a way through the mines. Look for it!"

"Will do."

Emmy drove his tank along the field while the others waited.

"Battalion commander, Eitan here. I suggest that Amnon and I look for a way through on the left flank."

"Okay. Good idea. But move carefully. If you find it, report immediately."

I wasn't used to standing and waiting, but I knew I had to be patient. Meanwhile, tanks of Emmy and Amnon's companies were firing at Syrian vehicles that had appeared on a ridge 1,500 yards ahead. Ben-Hanan reported to Yanosh that he was across and was passing the first houses of Jubata el-Hashab. I felt uncomfortable. Clearly it was going to take a lot longer to get my battalion over the mines—and it would have been different had the two support tanks functioned properly.

Emmy was steering through the trees with difficulty. Amnon, leading the search at his end, suddenly rolled over a mine in the unmarked area and shed a track. Transferring to another tank, he kept on looking.

"Emmy to battalion commander. I've found it."

"Very good. Cross cautiously and alone. The others follow when you're across safely."

We crossed, but it took too long a time. I heard over the brigade radio that Ben-Hanan was well ahead. His tanks were already approaching the road to Tel Amar. Yanosh would probably order a change of plan any moment now.

"I'm continuing east," Ben-Hanan reported. "Request artillery be moved 300 meters eastward."

Ben-Hanan was doing his own artillery liaison through brigade because his gunnery officer had been wounded minutes before.

"Confirmed," replied Yanosh. "When the artillery lifts, you are free to move. I'm sending in another unit behind you to move left."

Obvious. Tel Amar would be taken from south to north, using the Jubata road.

"I can hit Kahalani's area from the road."

"I know. Yos will do that. Yos, brigade commander here. Change of plan. You move on the axis of the road, and assault northward."

"Okay."

Emmy was ploughing through scrub and trees, smashing them down as he went. On top of the foliage, he was now on a steep downward slope, trying to get into the valley that would lead us to target. Eitan and Amnon had crossed the minefield and were following in our tracks. With the column strung out on tough ground, there was no alternative but to make decisions based only on what I heard over the battalion radio—a situation not at all to my liking.

"Kahalani, brigade commander here. What's your situation?"

"Advancing towards the Tel. It's hard going."

"Are tanks firing at you?"

"No. Destroyed most of them from our positions before we advanced."

"Good. I'm putting Yos into your sector. Coordinate with him."

"Right. I'll try to give him cover. If Yos is already on the road, he'll arrive before me because we have difficulties."

The idea that Yos would reach our target first wasn't pleasant, yet there could be no better decision under the circumstances. Meanwhile, we were proceeding in column, expecting to encounter Syrian infantry. Eitan reported that he and Amnon were beginning to climb the Tel. I tried to see them, but trees obscured the view.

Over the brigade frequency, I heard that Yos was having trouble in crossing the minefield. Ben-Hanan's tanks and sapper platoon were still blocking the way. Yos sounded excited. Yanosh ordered him to drop a soldier from one of the tanks to guide all the vehicles off the track and let him pass. That was some encouragement; now we might get there before him. Finally Yos reported that he was through and turning onto the road to the Tel.

"Battalion commander, Eitan here. Tanks are firing at me from the south."

"Yos. Cease fire! Cease fire! My tanks are on the Tel."

The thought of our tanks being hit by other members of the brigade was enough to send ice down my spine.

"Yos. Brigade commander here. Cease fire. Our own forces are on the Tel ... Yos! Yos! Acknowledge. Over."

"We have ceased fire," he said at last.

It still didn't feel right. Eitan and Amnon claimed to be on the Tel. I asked for a report on their location, and they said, "Nearing the peak." I couldn't see them, though the peak was in plain view.

Between Yos and Ben-Hanan trying to coordinate their moves, and Amos mistakenly calling his company commanders over the brigade frequency, it was beginning to sound like utter chaos.

"Brigade stations, commander speaking. Orders. Over."

I gathered that he must be wanting to restore order. One by one, he accepted reports from the battalions, then issued special instructions he had for the next stage.

"Kahalani, report."

"My deputy and a company have made a wide left sweep. From their reports—since I don't have them in view—they are on the approaches to target.

"Good. And you?"

"I'm 800 yards from target, still among the trees. A few more minutes, and I'll be in position to see and report precisely."

"Repeat. Didn't understand. Over."

"I repeat. My deputy and another company are on approaches to target. I'm moving towards it with a company. I still don't know exactly where my deputy is. Hold. I'll check with him and report."

I answered Yanosh patiently, though this was no time for debriefings. I would prefer to wait a few minutes till I could see for myself, but he persisted.

"Which target are you talking about?"

"Tel Amar."

"Are your forces on the Tel?"

"Yes. Not on the peak, but on the right flank."

"Are you in control of the crossroads?"

I misread the Hebrew "crossroads" (*tzomet*) for "crew" (*tzevet*), and decided to answer angrily.

"I'm still in the trees. It's difficult to observe, but I do have control over every tank."

"Fine, but I mean the crossroads—Tel Amar crossroads. I know you have control over your forces."

"Hold. I'll report immediately."

I intended to check with Eitan. As I appraised the situation, we didn't yet control the crossroads.

"Brigade commander here. Should we send Amos after you?"

"Negative."

Yanosh tried to hold Amos, but it was too late. He was already moving and couldn't turn in this terrain to head for the southern, more easily traversable, crossing.

Coming out of the trees was a great relief. I could see the entire force. The area at the foot of Tel Amar was ploughed ground, and a track led directly to the Tel. Eitan and Amnon had reached the peak, and Emmy now tacked on to their tail. Tanks were firing machine-gun bursts into communications trenches and an occasional shell at bunker openings. At first we saw no enemy tanks, then found four shiny and clean T-55s, abandoned in their firing positions. Once on the top, unarmed Syrian soldiers suddenly appeared, some of them with their arms up over their heads. Wary of surprises, I kept my 0.3 machine gun aimed at them. There were perhaps twenty-five soldiers under the command of a major. Seeing my gun, and looking scared out of their wits, they stood still, then obeyed my gesture to squat on the ground, their hands on their heads.

I reported my haul to Yanosh and was told not to let it delay me. As Yanosh called for an interrogator, I ordered Emmy to leave one tank to guard the prisoners. A little later, I recalled the tank to the battalion and detached two of Lutski's APCs of mechanized infantry to guard the prisoners, until someone arrived to evacuate them.

Tel Amar—the "red tel"—was in our hands. It had obviously been prepared as a strongpoint, complete with trenches, bunkers, tanks and stacks of ammunition. The whole lot appeared abandoned; I should perhaps put a shell into each bunker, but the ranges were too close and I didn't want to hit our prisoners.

"Eitan. Battalion commander here. I want you in position facing north and northeast, to engage the tanks on the ridge."

"Immediately."

" 'Policeman' stations. Battalion commander here. Open fire at long range as necessary."

Switching to brigade frequency, I reported to Yanosh that Tel Amar was secure. He was trying to send up an infantry force to clean out the bunkers and take charge of the prisoners, but they were still well behind. I decided not to wait. Raful chose that moment to cut into the brigade frequency and ask how things were going. Yanosh reported that Tel Amar was in our hands without any particular problems.

"We're laying a road," Raful said, referring to a special force that would link up our road system with the Syrian, so that vehicles without front-wheel drive could cross.

I took station on top of the Tel and surveyed the terrain. All our objectives were clearly visible, complete with access roads. It seemed simple. A road ran down the Tel and on to a crossing, where one branch led back towards Israel and the other on to Mazrat Beit Jan. I could pick out bunkers, from which anti-tank guns projected, and tanks, APCs and trucks in dug-outs—all pointed in the same direction, and all obviously placed to prevent any advance towards Mazrat Beit Jan.

Snir, standing beside me, started to guide artillery fire down on our next line of targets, according to an order of priorities that I gave him. Alongside the artillery, our own tanks were sniping at targets below us. Because of our elevated position, the ranges seemed short, but were in fact between 2,000 and 4,000 yards. I reflected that we had sustained no casualties so far and hoped that it would continue to be so up to Mazrat Beit Jan. Snir's targeting was good, and we could see Syrian soldiers running off into the trees. The enemy tanks that we could see were going up in flames, and Snir's artillerymen were scoring hits on the anti-tank bunkers. In any case, we had the advantage.

Those anti-tank guns were only good up to 1,200 yards, while our tank guns were accurate up to 2,500 yards.

Brigade radio was now busy coordinating between Yanosh, Ben-Hanan and Yos. I was free to operate independently, choosing my own tactics without external interference.

I could hear Raful asking Yanosh to speed up the link with Tel Dahur, in the direction of the central road to Damascus. Yos and Ben-Hanan remained on their sector, while Amos was now following me.

Thinking over how to take the next fortified position, I decided to leave a covering force on Tel Amar and to attack along the road with two companies. Amnon was in a good position to fire on the target. Emmy had led the battalion in the breakthrough. So I now decided to give Laor the point.

"Laor, battalion commander here. Form up in column, and be ready to move forward."

"Laor here. Acknowledged."

" 'Policeman' stations," I said, resolving to issue my orders by the book. "For the attack, Amnon will remain in covering positions. Laor and Emmy together will assault along the road towards Mazrat Beit Jan."

The company commanders acknowledged. Then I ordered Laor not to lead the column, but to take station in the first platoon. I didn't want the whole column halted in case the company commander stopped the first shell, and no one behind had the initiative to bypass the lead tank.

Laor issued orders to his vehicles, but it wasn't easy for him to choose the line-up in the column, since he didn't yet know all his men. Finally, unable to pick out a platoon leader, he took the front spot for himself and reported that he was ready to move. I ordered Snir to stay put on the Tel and to direct the artillery on target, yet to divert whenever he could to supply a rolling barrage in front of the assault column.

"Battalion commander here. Move out!"

As Laor's tanks jolted forwards, Eitan slid into the company column, apparently scared that I would order him to stay behind with Amnon. Emmy and I also inserted ourselves in the long line of tanks and headed for the next target. At first it was downhill going with no need to open fire. Abandoned trucks stood on the road and had to be avoided. It all seemed too slow to me, so I told Laor to increase the pace to a maximum.

The tanks were firing shells at random and pouring machine-gun bursts into communication trenches along the roadside. In this kind of advance, you keep firing even if you can't see a target. It keeps the enemy's head down and causes shock—which might be vital if you only have one axis on which to move. I fired my own machine gun at the trees, while Gidi tossed hand grenades into the trenches, until I told him to stop. It was a pity to waste the grenades.

The pace was now fast, with occasional stops as Laor took aim at tanks or APCs that stood in our way, or as we slid off the road to bypass abandoned Syrian vehicles. Then one of our tanks hit a mine, and its crew switched to another vehicle. As we rolled past, I noticed that the damaged tank was Eitan's; he was low on luck—this was his fourth change of tank since the war started.

"Laor, battalion commander here. Be careful of the tank ridge on your left flank."

I knew there were tank positions on the ridge, and according to our intelligence briefings, they were manned. The ridge was too far from Tel Amar for Amnon to do anything about it.

"Laor here. It's okay. I'm hitting them all the time."

Our advance along the road, fast as it was, had become a little frightening. The tanks were firing mercilessly right and left. Shells were bursting between the vehicles. Much as I tried, I couldn't identify the source of fire, though it seemed to be direct targetting from enemy tanks. We were exposed, but speed and our own fire to the flanks was granting a kind of immunity. In the middle of all this, Yanosh asked for a report. I told him we were continuing and that I would get back to him later.

"Battalion commander, Emmy here. There are enemy tanks on the left. Recommend we halt and hit them."

"Keep moving till we reach controlling ground."

"Battalion commander, Amnon here. I have nothing more to do up here. Am joining you."

"Alright. Move fast!"

"Battalion commander, Eitan here. Recommend Laor halt and allow rear tanks to group."

"I leave it to your judgment to choose the place. Meanwhile, it's going well, and we mustn't stop. Hope you're well. I saw you switched tanks."

"Yanosh, Raful here," the brigade radio cut across our conversation. "Most important that you press south. Most important that you reach the main road to Damascus."

"Yanosh here. Am going the maximum to reach the road."

Yanosh began to push Yos and Ben-Hanan. Meanwhile, I was running my own private war. Occasionally Amos would ask how I was doing, and where I was, since he was following. I could understand his feelings. He was passing through scorched earth, finding that the job had already been done.

"Kahalani, Amos here. What's your situation?"

"Target in my hands. Deployed to northeast."

"I'm following. Tanks are firing from the flanks, but I can't answer. I'm not sure of identification and location. Look to the south and north!"

"You fire south. I'll deal with the north," I said.

I switched back to the battalion radio.

"Laor, battalion commander here. I want you to take a dominating ridge and hold. I'm coming up to take a look ahead."

"The area ahead is mostly good. I'll stop immediately."

"Careful. Don't tangle with an enemy ambush."

I felt that I had to move up and dictate the next move. A mad rush down the road might bring us straight into a trap. These trees and trenches could conceal anti-tank guns. The air was full of smoke and cordite. The sun was behind our backs—a decided advantage.

"Kahalani, Yanosh here. Give your location."

"Difficult to say exactly. Seems that I have passed 'Hyena-China' crossroads."

This was the point of which we had been so wary—the point named Tank Ridge because of its preponderance of armor. While we were talking, some of my tanks had moved off the road to right and left to fire at anti-tank positions and tanks standing among the trees, even though they appeared to be abandoned. I had given permission for a move up to 200 yards from the road.

I've been compelled to leave the axis and comb right and left, but we're moving back and continuing to a ridge farther ahead to take a look."

"Congratulations, Kahalani. You're moving in an area where on both sides there are . . . You know what I mean."

I didn't, but I assumed he was still worried about minefields.

"I'm rolling. It's been tough so far. We've been under fire from tanks and anti-tank guns, but the men have performed very well, and we've destroyed our opposition. Anyway, I'll soon take position and let you know exactly where we are."

"Amos, brigade commander here. Kahalani is in the area of 'China-Hyena' crossing."

"Amos here. I see him. He's assaulting a place where there are tanks, and I can help him."

"He'll finish it alone."

Yanosh went on to instruct Amos to comb the area close to the road, as insurance that it wouldn't close behind us.

Laor stopped, and his tanks took positions to left and right. I moved up to a high spot and took a look eastward. Nothing special. So I ordered Laor to move on cautiously. He reached another ridge and again waited for me. Before my eyes was the village of Mazrat Beit Jan. I couldn't believe it, but the map confirmed the fact.

"Laor, battalion commander here, nice work!"

He smiled and waved to acknowledge the message. The village was in a green valley, amid thick foliage. Compared with what we had seen so far, this looked like a garden. The land was cultivated, and irrigated by a stream coming off the slopes of Mount Hermon. Beyond the village, I could see groves of fruit trees.

I ordered a move to bring us within closer range of the village. Laor took the north of the road, with Emmy to the south. It was slow going because of the basalt rocks. Finally we took up positions about 2,500 yards from the village and had a good look at it. The inhabitants were rushing around wildly. Some were carrying their belongings eastward. I reckoned we must give them time to run before we moved in. I tried to pinpoint the enemy in the village, but there was nothing to be seen. Satisfied on that score, we again moved forward to better positions.

"Kahalani, brigade commander here. Report situation."

"Am about three kilometers from final target. In my opinion, we can move in soon."

I was remembering that Raful stressed the importance of taking this village quickly.

"How far are you from the trees?"

"About three thousand."

"Have you got greens with you?"

"Don't understand what that is."

"Infantry."

"No. They remained near the frontier. I have no contact with them."

"Is the road open up to where you are?" Yanosh asked, apparently having difficulty in believing that we were already so close to success.

"It has been for some time," I replied confidently.

Yanosh acknowledged, then ordered Amos to move up fast, leaving one company to secure the road. Amos confirmed. Then it was Yos' turn, because Amos had to wait for his infantry to catch up. Yos was ordered to link up with me by way of "Rotary" road and Harpa village. I was beginning to feel lonely; one battalion was deep inside Syria, with the rest of the brigade strung out to the rear.

As we watched the village, we came under artillery fire. At first the shells fell near the tanks, then among us. I looked for the source and finally spotted it at some distance behind the village. Yanosh was still inquiring about my situation, though he was worried about Ben-Hanan and Yos.

"I have the feeling that I'll soon be giving you regards from the mayor."

Amos was given permission to shoot up the apparently abandoned tanks along the road. It seemed a pity to me; we could probably put them to good use. I tried to raise him on the radio to suggest that he should reconsider, but couldn't make contact.

"Kahalani, Yanosh here, how are things?"

I tried to answer, but too many people were interrupting on the brigade frequency.

Angrily I said, "Can't get a word in edgewise. I'm on the approaches to the village. I can take it or seize positions outside. As you please."

"Wait for orders. Meanwhile, keep control of the area."

I felt secure where I was and felt that I could have Mazrat Beit Jan within minutes, though I was a little worried by the foliage, which could serve as cover for the Syrians. Yanosh and Raful were now busy on the radio, and Yanosh was receiving permission to discontinue the advance along the main Damascus road. Dan Laner's division had broken through and no longer needed assistance from Ben-Hanan's battalion.

"You are free to concentrate on Mazrat Beit Jan. Is anybody already there?"

"Yes. Two thousand yards from the village and firing."

"Okay. Take the place. Take greens with you. You must have greens."

"That's good, but they're delayed, and I don't know why. It'll be alright."

26

OCTOBER 11, 1973 EVENING

A shell hit one of the tanks next to me. It needed no effort to
see the Syrians coming out of the trees south of the village. We
dropped into firing positions and watched the Syrians retire after
firing a few shells. I issued orders to fire if any of them reap-
peared. As each came out to fire, all our guns targeted on it.
Within minutes five Syrian tanks were pouring black smoke into
the sky. The others hid among the trees, presenting a danger
to any movement we might make towards the village. I wanted
artillery, but our guns were far behind, so we fired a few more
shells into the trees from where we were standing. With the sun
behind our backs, we had a good view of the village, and I
prepared to advance in leapfrog stages. I arrived with Amnon
at the forward line, 550 yards from Mazrat Beit Jan. One of his
tanks was hit, and the crew boarded another vehicle. I strained
to see the Syrians among the trees, but it was useless.

Yanosh was pressing me to take the village and set up a line
east of it. We decided that I should stay in position while Amos
moved through the village and out to the east. I issued orders
to the battalion, then waited for Amos. His first tanks arrived,
pulled into line with me and joined in the barrage on the village.
Then we spotted more Syrian tanks racing forward into the
village. The situation was becoming messy. Minutes later four
enemy helicopters landed in Mazrat Beit Jan, no doubt with
infantry.

"Yanosh, Kahalani here. It seems to me that the Syrians aren't
going to give up the village that quickly. Four helicopters have
just landed, and more tanks have come in from the east."

"We'll let them have artillery."

"I've tried that, but the range is too far for them. We need air."

"Alright. I'll take care of it."

We settled down to fire at will—one tank firing while a second spotted for it. I wasn't satisfied with the marksmanship. Apparently the crews had got too used to short-range work during the containment battles and were getting sloppy with the rules of gunnery. After a few roars of simulated rage and some nasty comments to the company commanders, the quality of fire improved.

Green-painted Syrian tanks still huddled in the foliage, making it difficult to spot them. On the other hand, we were exposed, and our advantage lay in the sun behind our backs, so we were only visible as shadows. I moved back a little to a better firing position. Now my tank was completely exposed, and I prodded Yuval to speed up, but the basalt rock made it hard going. Syrian tanks were firing salvoes at us. Suddenly I felt my temper rise. I plunged down into the turret and yelled to Yuval to step on the gas and ignore the obstacles. A shell whistled overhead. I knew that if we didn't get into position soon, that Syrian gunner would adjust his aim—and the next shell would hit us. Yuval got the message. He slammed down hard, and we dropped behind some dead ground. I began to breathe more freely. There was no point trying to hit the Syrian. Aiming and firing when not in a firing position is dangerous, wasteful, and stupid.

My thoughts slipped back to another similar incident....

On June 5, 1967, I was ordered by the brigade commander, Colonel Shmuel Gonen (Goradish), to attack the Rafia crossroads together with the second company I had along with me. I didn't have contact with the battalion commander, Ehud; the order came through by hand signals. Oved's company was behind me and to my right. First we straightened out the line, and then we began to advance. I didn't see the target, but a few minutes later we reached the first trench in the area of the crossroads, with hundreds of Arab heads peeking out of it and watching us in terror. The frightened soldiers began to flee as we came up behind them, moving slowly, with our machine guns firing away relentlessly. A few minutes later, as the assault continued, a shell exploded about 6 feet in front of me. I glanced quickly to the right and saw a T-34 tank firing from a position, its turret standing out prominently and its barrel pointing straight at my tank. I dove into the turret.

The cannon on my Patton wasn't working because of the crash that morning, and we were a sitting duck for the Egyptian. My driver put on speed as I searched for a dip in the ground where we could hide, but the whole area was flat and exposed. I waited for the second shell that was sure to come. Getting on the net, I directed the other tanks to the T-34 on my right and urged them to hit it quickly. Seconds later one of our tanks put a shell into the Egyptian. After that, I never stopped drumming into my students the lesson that whoever shoots faster and better lives longer.

Yanosh sounded angry and helpless. Ben-Hanan reported enemy tanks in Holes Camps. He was ordered to destroy them. He later reported that they seemed to be ours.

"Now I don't understand anything," Yanosh muttered.

Ben-Hanan and Yos were having identification problems—the result of fighting on the move. Their axes of advance took them through areas where the enemy had been reported. Yanosh was trying to keep up with each new location, but communications weren't functioning properly. He made use of Yos' deputy, Major Yossi, to try to pinpoint the battalion's position, and Yos and Ben-Hanan finally succeeded in coordinating.

At Mazrat Beit Jan, the situation was worsening. The Syrians were bringing up reinforcements and seemed determined to hold the village. Five more of their tanks found the courage to come out of the foliage and seek firing positions, though it was foolhardy on their part. They didn't last many minutes.

"Kahalani, Yanosh here. Report situation."

"They're reinforcing the village all the time. We've destroyed at least ten tanks. A battle is developing and delaying us."

"Your situation in the field?"

"At the moment, I'm in firing positions and improving the location because of the tanks that face me. Amos seems ready."

Kilyon yelled and took aim at an enemy tank.

"Hold a moment, I'm firing ..." Then I resumed, "We must have air on the village immediately."

"I'm trying to do that," said Yanosh, sounding a little apologetic at not having kept his earlier promise.

"In any event, we're on top, and the situation will remain in our favor, no matter how much they reinforce. If they bring in large-scale forces, we can make mishmash of them with artillery. It'll turn into a trap. Right now the problem is their tanks, and we have to deal with them while they're among the trees. They are difficult to spot, but we're returning their fire."

"I'm relying on you on your sector. You run things. I can't get there for the moment."

I could understand how Yanosh felt. In any case, his decisions were in consultation with me, and he depended on the judgments of Amos and me. Therefore, it was essential that we reported accurately and fully.

"Yanosh, Raful here. In a few minutes, you'll have air on the village."

"Thank you."

Yanosh sounded as happy as I felt. I ordered the battalion to put up markers for our aircraft.

The sun was beginning to sink behind our backs. We needed to take the village, but it would be dangerous with Syrian armor and infantry in possession. Any attempt would be at a heavy cost. Even if we succeeded, we would be sitting with tanks in darkness, in a wooded and built-up area, without infantry for guard duties and mopping up. That could be a terrible trap. I decided for the time being to keep up the pressure from outside the village. Amos told me that he was ready to go, under cover of my fire, but I resolved to wait.

Raful solved the problem.

"Yanosh. Take note. No need to break our heads and get killed over the village. We don't need to pass it. We have to hold the Kort-Mosque crossing."

That was right below us, between our tanks and the village, and we already controlled it.

Yanosh didn't get the message, so Raful repeated with an addition:

"We don't need to smash ourselves on the village, though according to my reports, there are only ten tanks there."

I felt a little insulted at that, nevertheless I didn't interrupt the division commander.

"Take positions and bring up infantry to secure your hold."

Somebody must have been blocking the radio, for Yanosh still didn't acknowledge.

"I repeat, there's no need to smash ourselves on the village. It's enough to hold the Kort-Mosque crossing. We'll give you all we can. Am sending up infantry to hold and to protect you. My neighbor to the south [Dan Laner] is already at Tel Shams."

Yanosh did not relay Raful's orders to us because Ben-Hanan was screaming into the radio that he was being fired at by our tanks. It turned out that Yos' machine guns had mistakenly fired at Ben-Hanan. Yanosh straightened that out, then instructed Yos to take Harfa. After that, he contacted me for a consultation on the next moves, on the assumption that I had heard Raful's orders. Finally, he told me to stay put but be ready to move on Harfa if Yos didn't succeed.

By now the sun was down and we had disengaged from the Syrians. We encamped for the night. Amos was behind me near the Mazrat Beit Jan road, and my tanks were close to our new firing positions. We towed our disabled tanks into camp. A company of infantry arrived on half-tracks, with their deputy battalion commander, and fanned out to cover the weak points. I had been waiting for the infantry to set up defenses at some distance away from the tanks. We were about 2,750 yards from the Syrians, in an area covered with foliage and creased by gullies. We expected bazooka raids during the night. The infantry around us gave me a good feeling, though I could not relax our own alert. After ordering a sentry on each tank and continuous monitoring of the radios, I called in the company commanders and Eitan to brief them on the morrow's moves.

I didn't know whether we would finally go into Mazrat Beit Jan, but to be on the safe side, I briefed them on how to go about any mission that might develop. That over and done with, we all stayed on the tank, swapping notes on the day's events. We were in high spirits. The fact that we had sustained no casualties on our first day inside Syria did much for our morale.

I decided to spend my first night inside Syria catching up on lost sleep. My crew washed and changed underwear and socks.

"Sir, we have some for you, too," said Kilyon, holding out sparkling white underwear and new socks. The temptation was too great. I accepted, and it felt wonderful. With the dust and cordite washed off my face, I was a new man, even though my stubble was already making the beginnings of a beard.

Before finally turning in for the night, I called Eitan to ask him to take charge of fuel and ammunition. He reported that the supply convoy was already on its way. Then I settled down on the commander's seat and fell asleep. Nothing happened till early morning. From time to time, I stirred and looked around. Men were moving around, and somebody was obviously alert.

At 0300 hours, I was awakened by the noise of vehicles on the road. I tried to identify them by moonlight. They seemed to be trucks of ours heading for the village.

"Who are they?" I asked Gidi, who was standing in the loader/ radioman's cupola.

"I don't know."

"What! Then who does?"

"Perhaps it's the fuel and ammunition convoy."

"They're not here yet?"

"They were held up a long time with Amos," said Gidi, noticeably unable to understand what I was so excited about. Excited? No! Furious! Through the telescope, I watched them drive on towards Mazrat Beit Jan, and had visions of them ending in an inferno of Syrian fire.

"Are they on our radio frequency?"

"Yes. I spoke to them minutes back," said Gidi, then continued as if knowing what my next question would be. "The convoy is led by the brigade intelligence officer, Captain Menahem."

I had to stop them—fast.

"Brigade intelligence officer, Kahalani here. Stop! Stop immediately!"

There was no response.

"Stop! Stop immediately! We're already behind you."

Still no response. The trucks merely picked up speed down the incline to the village.

"Prepare to move," I yelled at the dumbfounded Gidi, "I want us up in firing position fast."

He didn't grasp the purpose of such a strange order at this hour of night. But all I could see was a slim chance that we might be able to protect the trucks.

"Brigade intelligence officer, stop! Stop!"

It was a final yell of desperation.

"I'm stopping. I'm stopping."

I sighed with relief. The lead truck was now 400 yards from the village.

"Listen, my friend, we are behind you. Turn around carefully, then head back fast. The enemy is ahead of you and might open fire any minute."

I spoke quietly but stressed the last sentence.

"Alright. I'm returning."

His voice was calm; he had no fear—and perhaps no real understanding of his predicament. I watched them as more trucks joined the tail, then turned around with agonizing slowness.

After long moments of tension, the trucks arrived at our camp. We now lacked for nothing: fuel, ammunition, battle rations including fresh cakes, vegetables and fruit—and newspapers that indeed confirmed that Israel was at war. There were also five transistor radios, which we divided among the companies.

27

OCTOBER 12, 1973   MORNING

Dawn. I didn't know what the new day would bring. I deployed the tanks in their positions facing the village. It was preferable to open fire before the sun came up, because it would be in our faces, and we might not be able to identify our targets. We loaded a shell.

"Battalion commander, I can see a Syrian tank among the foliage. Am asking permission to fire," Amnon called.

He was standing to my left. Military discipline was still binding my men, and the commander's permission to fire the first shot of the day was part of it.

" 'Policeman' stations, battalion commander here. Anyone who spots an enemy is free to open fire, and I mean controlled and effective fire."

Almost instantaneously a shell erupted from Amnon's gun. It wasn't long before the whole orchestra was playing. The Syrians were also up early and were firing at us. We were feeling fine on the high ground, even though the advantage would soon be matched against the rising sun. The dazzling rays compelled us to drop down to observation positions where we could continue trying. The Syrian tanks kept on firing at our positions— an element that increased the tension. We began to take the game more seriously. Standing still, with little to do, I considered new ways to take advantage of our high ground.

To the north of us was a ridge overlooking the village. We had to have it if we wanted to pick out targets in the village despite the sun in our eyes. From that ridge, we would also have a view of the road from Mazrat Beit Jan to Beit Jan.

The Syrian barrage began at first on the area immediately behind us, now on our positions. Because we faced the sun, we could not tell where the shells were coming from. I ordered Emmy and Eitan up to the ridge to the north, together with Second Lieutenant Lutsky, who was to keep watch for incoming Syrian troops. I assigned Snir to locating the source of the enemy artillery barrage.

Some of Amos' tanks moved into line alongside us and added their fire on the village. As the sun rose in the heavens, we were no longer blinded. Our chilled bones thawed and the last webs of sleep were driven from our eyes. Now we could see ten tanks in position facing us. There had to be more of them in the village, but we couldn't pick them out yet. There was no sign of the infantry brought by helicopter, nor of the inhabitants of Mazrat Beit Jan. I reported to Yanosh, and he ordered us to take the village. That put us back with the plan of yesterday. Amos would go in while we covered him.

We had hit a number of tanks, and Snir was directing artillery fire on the village, raising "bonfires" behind a number of houses—but their guns were still raining down an accurate shower of shells.

Seeing that the situation was getting more complicated and that there were no signs of the Syrians breaking, I asked Yanosh for air strikes on the village. Within twenty minutes, four Skyhawks were dropping their bombs between the houses and trees, each hit causing a pillar of grey smoke. We stood watching the display, happy that the Syrian guns had stopped when our aircraft appeared. The planes left—and a shell promptly came to ground next to my tank, reminding us that the show was not over.

Suddenly I noticed Platoon Leader Amos Nahum a few yards away to my left, half-exposed in the turret and lifting a hand to ask for help. I couldn't hear him but could see that he was wounded.

"Doctor, battalion commander here. Come up immediately."

"I'm on my way."

Amos was down on his seat, and Second Lieutenant Noah Timienker—the fifth man in Amnon's tank—was running over to him. I knew that Amos would get the necessary assistance. His thigh was hit by shrapnel and was bleeding profusely. Natan and David, his crewmen, were bandaging the open wound, but

the bleeding didn't stop. Noah grabbed an 0.3 empty ammunition belt and used it round the leg as a constricting band, and
that slowed the bleeding. The three placed Amos on an open
stretcher above the engine compartment. Doctor Alex raced up,
convinced that something had happened to my tank. He wasn't
used to being called by me. Transferring Amos to his APC, Alex
replaced Noah's improvisation by a proper arterial tourniquet
and gave him two transfusions. The color in his face returned,
and he began to feel better.

Noah climbed on to Amos' tank to take his place as commander, while Alex hurtled back to a rendezvous with a helicopter ordered from the brigade doctor.

"MiGs. MiGs!"

At the scream over the battalion radio, all the turret machine
guns swung upward and bursts were fired at the two intruders,
but without any luck. The planes, combined with artillery and
tanks, further confirmed that the Syrians had no intention of
handing over Mazrat Beit Jan. The tank fire had almost stopped,
since many of them were damaged and the others had opted to
break off contact and merely keep watch.

"Amos, I don't see any more tanks facing us. I think it would
be best to go in now."

"I'm making final preparations."

"I'll give you the best cover I can."

I felt a little uncomfortable about supplying covering fire while
Amos took the village. I was used to seeing my battalion do the
most dangerous work. But it was legitimate, since Amos' battalion hadn't yet carried out a major operation.

" 'Policeman' stations, battalion commander here. Pay attention. In a few minutes from now, Amos' battalion will be assaulting Mazrat Beit Jan. We will stay in our present positions
and supply covering fire."

I waited for the company commanders to acknowledge, then
continued.

"I want you to understand the significance of taking this place.
The assault will be along the road, and we are the only ones
who can prevent the enemy from blocking the attack. I want
anything that shows among the trees eliminated and neutralized."

Amos' tanks formed up on the road and began their race to

the village. The barrage moved away from us to the road where the assault force was moving. That they weren't hit was solely due to divine intervention. I had to admire the commanders and crews. Within seconds a quartet of Syrian MiGs were diving on the column and dropping their bombs.

As a commander and as an armor veteran, I was proud of this display of matchless courage. Nothing was stirring yet among the trees—only the artillery and aircraft—but the Syrians were being obstinate. On the other hand, I knew that once they reached the village, the tanks would be free of the barrage and bombing. The Syrians wouldn't fire on their own. The lead tank reached the last turn and raced into the village. This was where the big battle had to be, and I couldn't see the outskirts clearly because of a rise in the ground in front of me.

"Amos, Kahalani here."

I was using his battalion frequency to offer what encouragement I could.

"From where I am, it looks marvellous. But you mustn't stop. I believe the artillery and air will stop once you're all inside."

I didn't wait for acknowledgment. I knew he could hear me, and that was what mattered. Then Gidi hit my shoulder and screamed, "Get inside!" Without thinking, I ducked down, close behind him.

"Plane," he yelled, pressing up against the inner wall.

There was a tremendous explosion, the like of which I had never heard before, and the tank rocked on its tracks. I bunched up and closed my eyes tight in an attempt to protect myself against the buffeting. Now I felt fear of death—that same fear I had felt on previous occasions, yet each successive time it became sharper, more vivid. I opened my eyes but could see only dust and black smoke. I ran my hands down my body in an instinctive check that everything was in place. There were voices and coughing. No air to breathe inside the tank....

"Everyone prepare to jump out," I announced into the intercom.

The dust settled. First I identified Kilyon, then Gidi and Gideon. When I heard Yuval on the intercom, I knew that all was well.

"What was that?"

"Plane. I saw its bombs in the air."

"Good for you," I said to Gidi, then emerged to check the damage. There was a crater behind the tank, and another a little farther off. The air was still full of dust. Tank commanders were checking the damage done to their vehicles. Within seconds I had casualty reports. Avraham Snir, my artillery officer to my left, was killed instantaneously—his body hanging out of the tank. He hadn't time to get into the turret. Yehoshua Shtrenzi, his tank commander, lay lifeless—a metal splinter projecting from his forehead. Ofer Ben-Neriya, now the sergeant of Amnon's Number Two Platoon, was killed instantaneously.

I needed time to recover. I summoned the doctor and ordered the company commanders to continue covering Amos. Snir's loader/radioman asked what he should do.

"Guide the driver around, and follow me," I told the panic-stricken soldier.

I directed Yuval back out of our firing position and headed for the cover of some fig trees, about 100 yards away, followed by Amnon, Noah, Snir's tank and Ofer Ben-Neriya's. We pulled up side by side. Ofer was brought down by his crew and by Noah—always willing to help—and placed on a stretcher next to a stone wall, his body covered by a blanket. The doctor arrived to evacuate the dead.

My map table had been dislodged. All the personal equipment strapped to the tank was riddled with holes. Our sleeping bags were missing. A large hole had appeared in the bore evacuator of our main gun. Clearly, we would not be effective, since our shell velocity would be much reduced without proper gas deflection.

I tried to catch a glimpse of the battle for Mazrat Beit Jan, but we were too low down. Gideon and Kilyon set to work stripping the gas vent off Ofer's tank and assembling it on our own gun. I caught them at it a little later and didn't agree to the operation. To their astonishment, I said that I didn't make a habit of cannibalizing other tanks. I felt there was something wrong about stripping Ofer's tank, and—quite apart from that—I didn't want to change my tank or any part of it out of some kind of faith that I would succeed in finishing the war in my own vehicle. The two of them put back our own damaged gas vent, and we returned to position. I guided the tank back to our old spot and promptly saw my map, Gidi's torn helmet and our sleeping bags lying on the ground. Gidi jumped down to collect the treasures. I clipped the map back into place, even though it had been torn in an unimportant corner. There was a deep rent in my sleeping bag, not that that would stop me using it for the rest of the war.

Amos' battalion was in the village, and I didn't know what was happening. I called him a few times on the brigade frequency, but he didn't answer. Switching to his battalion wavelength, I caught snatches of conversation between his company commanders about their difficulties. Again I called Amos, still without answer. Something must have happened to him. Finally his operations officer responded.

"Where's Amos?"

"Wounded in the head. He's being treated now."

"Bad wound?"

"I don't know yet. I want to evacuate him, but have no possibility. Can you help?"

"I'll send my doctor."

I broke off for a moment to instruct Alex, then returned to Amos' frequency.

"I want to know what's happening in there."

"We're inside the village. There's firing and explosions."

"Are you in control of the entire village?"

"I have to check that."

"I don't understand. Weren't you with the battalion commander?"

"I'm on a half-track, travelling independently."

"I'll wait for your answer."

A few minutes later, he told me that he only had contact with one company commander, who said he was pinned down; every tank that tried to cross the road was hit by a Syrian gun.

"It seems to me that you must take command," I said.

I understood that the battalion didn't have a deputy commander.

"I'll make contact with the companies immediately and report to you what happens," he said.

"I'll be waiting for the report on my frequency. Incidentally, are we acquainted?" I asked.

"Avi," replied a peeved voice, "this is Amos. We were to-gether in Jackie's unit."

"Amos Lurie?"

"Yes."

"Are you mad? What are you doing there?"

"What everybody else is doing."

Amos Lurie had been wounded in the War of Attrition—a large chunk of shrapnel had amputated his hand. He had left the Army and gone to study at Tel Aviv University. Neverthe-less, he was here. . . .

Minutes later Amos was back to report that he was putting some kind of order into the battalion. I tried to raise Alex and find out how the other Amos—the battalion commander—was faring, but without any luck. I decided to take command myself because I was worried that the battalion was getting deeper into a trap.

28

OCTOBER 12, 1973   AFTERNOON

I talked to each of the company commanders, clarifying their situation and telling them what to do. The operations officer kept me informed about anti-tank ambushes and the Syrian guns that kept the crews in column within the village. I suggested to Amos that a few men drop off the tanks and attempt to take care of the enemy guns from the ground on foot, but the mission didn't materialize because of a new interruption; a company answering to "Rainy Day" (*Sagrir*) arrived at the village to rejoin Amos' battalion—its parent unit.

"Who are you?"

"I was sent on a special assignment to Beit Jan. Have just completed it, and want to rejoin my battalion. Where is it?"

"Inside the village. Wait. Don't go in. I'll guide you," I cautioned.

There was no point in bogging down another company on a narrow road. Emmy and Eitan were reporting tanks to the east of the village firing at Amos' force.

" 'Rainy Day,' Kahalani here. Try to enter the village from the south—not by the main road."

" 'Rainy Day' here. I don't quite understand what you mean."

By now I could see his tanks off to my right on the road. By means of hand signals, I directed the company commander to make a sweep in from the south. When he reached the grove of trees, I ordered him to go through it in a northerly direction. Eitan and Emmy helped give him information about the Syrian tanks they could see behind the trees. The 'Rainy Day' commander seemed to be bold and forceful—apparently a battle-experienced veteran. As he was approaching the ploughed land beyond which the Syrians were standing, they began to advance and the tension rose.

" 'Rainy Day,' Kahalani here. Pay attention to the grove two hundred yards north of you. Five or so Syrian tanks have just entered it. Be ready to engage them!"

"I'm preparing for targetting immediately."

"Now, start moving, because you're on open ground and they're likely to fire at you from between the trees. I repeat, go in cautiously."

We were all tense. 'Rainy Day's' tanks went into the grove and vanished from view. I knew we would see fires among the trees any minute now, and sure enough, one after the other, there they were—pillars of black smoke. But whose tanks were burning? For a moment, I hesitated to ask, then I found the courage to call 'Rainy Day.'

"I'm okay. We've destroyed four tanks."

"Well done. Continue to be careful."

"Avi, stop worrying."

I was stunned. Who could it be this time? From Emmy's and Eitan's positions, they could open fire on the Syrian tanks to the north of the village. I gave permission, but only when I was sure that they were enemy. They were firing armor-piercing and were quickly joined by 'Rainy Day's' guns. Again I plucked up the nerve to ask who he was.

"Avi, it's Dror."

"Menahem Dror?" I asked hesitantly.

"That's right."

"You want to tell me you came from America for this party?"

"I was lonesome for you."

Now I could hear the familiar laugh.

"And who let you on a tank?"

"Do you think anyone was paying attention?"

"Dror, good for you. I'm proud to have friends like you. Look after yourself."

Dror had been badly wounded in the chest and head during the Six-Day War. Brought to the hospital at the very last moment, he had been lucky to stay alive. The doctors weren't convinced about his mental balance because of the head injury, but he insisted on going back to work. His superiors posted him to an instructor's job at the Armor School. Then one Friday night he felt an odd twitch in his head. Whatever had been wrong was gone; his self-confidence was fully restored overnight, yet the doctors wouldn't permit him to board a tank again on the contention that he might have a relapse. His contract with the Army wasn't renewed. After a long and losing battle for recognition as a disabled soldier eligible for help to study, he gave up and went to the United States to complete a university education.

Dror destroyed the tanks in the grove—and I knew that Mazrat Beit Jan was ours. What remained now was to group the force in the village against a Syrian offensive. Amos, the operations officer, reported that the damage to their tanks had all been the work of one Syrian. The problem was over, and we could deploy. I suggested that each company commander be given a clearly defined sector and that the force should prepare to secure its area. I inquired about Amos, the battalion commander, but his namesake couldn't give me any details. The doctor later told me that the wounded Amos had refused evacuation and was lying— his head in bandages—alongside the medical team's APC, but the men of his battalion knew nothing about it.

I moved Amnon's company on to high ground 200 yards from the village, and Eitan chose to go with him. Later on I gave them permission to enter the village to see what was going on. Eitan reported that all was quiet and that the other battalion was beginning to organize itself.

I very much wanted to go down, but still expected a counterattack and knew the importance of my job outside the village. From my vantage point, I could see for miles around Mazrat Beit Jan, and that was our protection against surprise attack, but I was afraid we were going to have to move southward, since brigade was reporting signs of a new attack. That being the case, I decided to take a quick look at Mazrat Beit Jan. Telling the company commanders to keep a watch in all directions and report anything untoward, I drove down to meet Eitan at the entrance to the village. The road down was gashed by tank tracks and pitted by shellfire and bombs. One of the Syrian tanks seemed intact, perhaps ready to fire a last desperate shell at us. I watched carefully for any sign of movement, but the gun barrel didn't budge. The air around the tanks was heavy with the smell of burning and of seared flesh.

We maneuvered between carob and mulberry trees, occasional grapevines, and flower beds—a pastoral scene that might have deluded us into forgetting that there was a war in progress. This place had a beauty and tranquility all its own, a veritable Garden of Eden.

Eitan was waiting beyond a bridge, noting my excitement as I came towards him.

"Beautiful, eh?"

"Very," I replied, signalling him to lead the way into Mazrat Beit Jan. Wooden shacks were still burning, and hysterical farm animals were racing round the courtyards, frightened by the din of tanks and the bursting shells.

Amos' tanks were spread out across the village. Eitan drove towards an open area alongside a mosque in the village center. We parked the tanks and set off on foot. Officers and men who knew me came over, all smiling. In conversation with them, I learned that they had all joined the war later—some straight from overseas, others because they could not find their units. I asked for Amos, the battalion commander, and was directed to one of the nearby houses. The tank that blocked the doorway was his. Skirting around it, I entered to find Amos poring over a map, trying to learn the terrain. He got to his feet and we shook hands. His head wound was not too deep, and he felt fine. The bandage wrapped around his forehead, and his hands, were stained with dried blood.

"What's the situation, Amos?"

"It'll be alright."

"What do you intend to do now?"

"I'm trying to plan our defense of the village. Come and help me do it."

"I don't expect to be here by evening. It's still hot over there with Ben-Hanan and Yos on the southern sector."

"I heard that Ben-Hanan was wounded," said Amos.

"When?"

"A few minutes ago."

"Seriously?"

"I don't know. I think I heard his voice on the radio."

I climbed aboard Amos' tank and listened to the radio. Ben-Hanan's attack on Tel Shams had failed, and he had indeed been wounded. I heard him asking for help but didn't know where he was calling from, or how he got a radio, since his tank had been hit. Later I found out that his tank was hit by a missile, and he was thrown clear with a severe leg injury. The turret personnel were killed. His driver jumped out, and the two of them hid in a foxhole. Some time later, the driver got back into the tank and removed the spare radio—and this was what Ben-Hanan used to call for help.

It was late afternoon. We were all afraid that some enemy infantry detail might get those two men alone in the field. Ben-Hanan and Yanosh were talking, using first names, and the latter sounded worried. I knew the two men were close friends ever since Yanosh was operations officer and Ben-Hanan was on the staff. The brigade commander now put together a small force, commanded by Major Yoni Netanyahu of the paratroops (who would be killed on July 4, 1976, leading the Entebbe rescue force) and—with the help of Yos' deputy—they collected Ben-Hanan and his driver. After a check to see that no other men were trapped in enemy territory, the force brought the two back for treatment and evacuation to a rear hospital.

The sun was slowly sinking as I left the village, having agreed to stay in touch with Amos and to continue to coordinate defense with him. I organized the battalion in night bivouac. Yanosh stayed in contact with us. Shortly before dark he asked whether we still needed the entire force. I replied that one battalion, supported by a detachment of infantry, would be enough to defend ourselves in the village, though I would have to leave a tank platoon to patrol the road—otherwise the garrison might easily be cut off since they were so deep in Syrian territory.

"Be ready to move in our direction—to 'Mosque' axis."

"Right."

I glanced at the map. "Mosque" was the route that linked Mazrat Beit Jan with "America" axis, which continued to Damascus. I knew we had Harfa village but did not know what force was there. Shortly after dark, Yanosh ordered me to move out fast. When I arrived at America-Mosque crossing, I would receive instructions.

While on the move, I heard Yanosh talking to Raful, and I began to understand the picture. Dan Laner's division had advanced along the Damascus road, widening our bulge towards Tel Antar and Nasaj. His force had been attacked, in the later afternoon, by a large enemy group that included tanks.

"They must be helped," Raful told Yanosh.

He sounded worried—and that surprised me.

"I'll do all I can. Kahalani is on the way, and I reckon I'll be placing him where we agreed within half an hour."

The two must have met earlier, or talked on the corps frequency. Raful had referred to "pox," but it meant nothing to me. Yanosh would refer to the term again in defining my mission.

"I don't understand what you mean," I said.

"I'm associating a force coming from the east with 'pox.' "

"Listen. It's still not clear to me. Does it make any difference to my deployment?"

"None at all. The important thing is that you move fast, then deploy for containment."

"Acknowledged."

"Perhaps 'pyjamas' tells you something," Yanosh suggested.

Now I understood. The Iraqi Army had joined the Syrians. "Pyjamas" was the trademark of the Iraqi Jews who had come to Israel in the 1950s and who had acquired their nickname because they spent the entire Sabbath day dressed in night dress.

"Alright. I have you now. But you've just reminded me that tomorrow is Saturday."

A few minutes later, we deployed to meet the Iraqi Army—though we would only meet them in the morning.

29

THE LAST DAYS:
OCTOBER 13-23, 1973

On Saturday, we settled down in good positions on what became the final lines of the bulge. We were now in a defense posture. The Syrians tried to bother us every day with artillery fire and abortive attacks.

One night during the week, the battalion adjutant arrived and presented me with a roster of battalion dead and wounded. I knew every name.

"Amir Bashari, Yair Swet, Yisrael Barzilai, Yoav Bluman . . . What? Yoav dead?"

"Yes."

"Where? When?"

"On the third or fourth day. Apparently he joined a reserve unit that was holding the Syrians at Nafah."

"Are you sure he was killed? Where's the information from?"

"It's a hospital list and it's precise."

All three of the friends gone—and I hadn't even known it. . . . I went on down the list of names.

"Avinoam Shemesh, Hai Herzl—Edri's loader—David Edri, Boaz Freedman . . ."

Boaz had wanted to change Freedman to a Hebrew name . . . Padan. Must check on that.

"Avihu Sandler, Amihai Doron, Avraham Snir, Amos Nahum . . . Can't be! Amos was only lightly injured."

"He got to the hospital and died there."

"But the doctor told me that he wasn't seriously wounded."

The last name was Ofer Ben-Neriya, killed together with Snir. On the list of wounded were names that I didn't know, but I was satisfied that someone was keeping a check and compiling the list. One name that did delight me was Yehoshua—Snir's tank commander. He was no longer on the critical list. But I was also reminded that I would have to do the rounds of the families to tell them something of what their men had been through. For the time being, I told the adjutant to take my car, which was standing in Rosh Pina, and the battalion intelligence officer, and start calling on the bereaved families to tell them that our thoughts were with them. I gave him a detailed briefing on how to behave and what to tell them. He had to be able to answer every question, but if he couldn't, he should say so loud and clear. Better that than invent stories. He would also need to learn about our battles and get some idea of where each of our dead fell. The trip was important. He had to realize that, and he had to tell them that both I and the company commanders would fill in the details later.

This I knew from experience. I knew they had to be visited during "Shiva," the seven-day mourning period, and that they would ask all kinds of questions about the last moments of their loved ones.

He spent three days, together with the intelligence officer and Yair's deputy, Lieutenant Dani Georgi, visiting most of the bereaved families.

We stood day after day in our positions under Syrian artillery fire. There was no way I could talk to all the men of the battalion. Then Yanosh withdrew us from the line to carry out maintenance on the tanks, while Amos replaced us. This was the opportunity. I ordered the company commanders to assemble the men.

Beginning with a survey of what was going on in the area, I gave them my assessment of coming developments. We already knew about Kissinger's efforts to achieve a cease-fire. Yet we were perturbed that it would take a long time. We needed quiet and rest above all else. Though the sector had been relatively peaceful the last few days, Syrian counterattacks were still possible. One thing that was troubling me—and I said so—was the relaxation of alertness in the tanks. The men were spending their free time to sleep—perhaps in their desire to escape reality—but I couldn't allow it. Finally I spoke about the need to write home. Kilyon admitted that he hadn't written a single letter because, he said, "I don't like writing." Later on I found out that he was afraid to write, having been told in a letter from his kibbutz about parents who had received a letter from their son, had relaxed, then forty-eight hours afterwards, got notice that the boy was dead. I checked on each and every one of them; some hadn't written.

"All of you will write a letter home today—and that's an order!"

I smiled and got an answering gale of laughter.

"Anyone who doesn't want to write can pack his kit and go home."

Towards evening I asked the company commanders to report any soldier who didn't write.

Night camp had become a meeting point with the home front: parcels, letters, food, ammunition and fuel. There were letters for boys who had been killed, and I asked that they be kept together till the war was over. One night I was handed a parcel addressed to Amir Bashari from Sara Bashari. Must be from his mother, I thought. The sergeant-major who brought it asked me what to do. The parcel was ripped, and we could see that it contained fruit. If it was returned, the fruit would rot—but if we divided it among the men, there would probably be a scandal, so back it went.

There were no letters for me (for reasons which I would learn later), but I did get messages from Dalia through people who phoned her. One night my driver came up with greetings from home. When he took the adjutant to visit the bereaved families, I asked him to call home and tell Dalia to get someone to fix the tiles on the unfinished roof—no matter what it cost. He returned to tell me that it had already been done. The head of the Local Council had ordered a Civil Defense man, who was a tiler by profession, to fix it. Now I could relax. My family wouldn't get wet.

When the supply convoy came up each night, the uproar was unbelievable. That was not at all to my liking, since the enemy was probably still interested in knowing our precise location, but the runners whom I sent with requests for silence did not do the trick. Finally I fired a long machine-gun burst into the air. A deadly silence descended, giving me the chance to announce, "If it does not stay silent, my next burst will be aimed at the center of the camp." I had made my point.

During one of the lulls between periodic Syrian bombardments, Menahem Dror jumped on my tank for a short visit.

"Avi, have you heard that Shalom Engel was killed?"

"What?" I shouted. "That can't be true."

"Yes. It's correct."

"How did it happen?"

"I think it was an accident on his way to the front."

Tears rolled down my cheeks, and a lump choked my throat. Dror put a hand on my shoulder. Luckily the radio was silent; I couldn't have spoken to anyone. Shalom and I had been close friends for many years. I was remembering how he brought me the news that Adam Weiler was dead. My friends were vanishing one by one.

When I awoke one morning, I could feel that my overalls were stuck to my thigh. A brief check disclosed that a piece of skin was missing from the back of my left thigh. I tried to find the reason for the wound and discovered that on the previous night I had fallen asleep near the motor, and the heat from the exhaust had caused a burn on my leg. I didn't feel it because most of the skin on my leg is numb to sensation. The wound was about the size of three postage stamps. I thought to myself that if Dr. Kaplan, my doctor in Beersheba, could see it, he would insist on an operation.

All the burns I suffered in the Six-Day War were third-degree. They were patched over and healed by twelve plastic surgery operations in which skin was transferred from healthy areas of my body to the charred parts. The healthy tissue was divided into pieces the size of a postage stamp and transplanted onto the burned areas. For a whole year, skin was being transplanted. During that time, I followed, day by day, how my wounds healed and transformed into numb scar tissue.

My stay in the hospital was the most trying test of my life. I went through hell there, though I tried not to show it. I didn't want to make things hard on my doctors, nurses, and especially my family. My wife, mother, and sister Ilana sat beside me day and night trying to make the suffering more bearable. Nevertheless, the experiences from the hospital are etched deep in my body. They will never disappear.

Now Dr. Alex and the infirmary sergeant, Sass, were eager to care for their battalion commander after days in which, fortunately, they were totally idle.

One night, while tired and half asleep, Eitan pressed the trigger of his machine gun by accident. His other hand happened to be over the barrel, and two bullets went though the palm of his hand. As I leaped on his tank, he was gripping his wounded hand, his face twisted up with pain. Within seconds he was bandaged and the bleeding had stopped.

"That was all I needed," he said in desperation and anger.

"Could happen to anyone. The important thing is you're alive."

"You know, I've been afraid all the time that someone would get hurt because of some stupidity, and now it's happened to me."

"Eitan, I hope it isn't serious. You'll be back in a few days. Meanwhile, you are wounded, and you have to be evacuated."

We smiled and parted. Some ligaments were torn and bones broken. He was hospitalized for quite a while. From that day on, I also took over battalion administrative affairs, dividing the load between Gidi and myself.

30

THE LAST 24 HOURS—
OCTOBER 24, 1973

In the late afternoon of October 23, I was sitting with the brigade staff in Yanosh's APC, trading experiences, sipping good coffee and nibbling cake. A cease-fire had been agreed upon the previous evening on the Egyptian front, but we heard that the fighting was continuing.

"The Syrians are as obstinate as ever, but I guess they'll ask for a cease-fire in a few days," Yanosh ventured.

"What's going on in Egypt?" I asked.

"I don't have details, but I know the Egyptians are screaming that our men across the Canal are hitting where it hurts. I imagine that the Syrians will repeat last night's desperate performance to get Tel Mar'i. Listen, Kahalani, you're sitting on that hill like a bone in their throats, and they must try to get it back."

"Do you know what happened last night? It was black. The men were seeing shapes everywhere, real and imaginary. This morning, it was only by luck that none of our tanks was hit when they started with their bazookas." A Syrian force, joined by Saudis and Iraqis, tried in vain to dislodge us from Tel Mar'i.

"Perhaps I'll be giving you infantry tonight."

"Infantry's fine, but I must have plenty of star shells."

"Aryeh is already dealing with it. Tonight you will have them."

"Kahalani," Haggai joined in, "your battle this morning was like an exercise. And, you know, I love to hear your accent on the radio. Your boys are imitating you, especially the way you say *Sof* [Hebrew for "end"]."

"Interesting. I hadn't noticed."

"How's morale in the battalion?" Yanosh wanted to know.

"Fine, at least I think so."

"I have a surprise for you. Tomorrow a new battalion is coming in to relieve you. You're pulling back to reorganize."

"You're kidding."

"I wouldn't kid you. You're moving back to Nafah for a few days. The whole brigade is coming out of the line."

"Who's relieving us?" I said, trying to hide my joy.

"They've reorganized Ben-Shoham's brigade."

"Excellent. I'm going back to pack."

"Kahalani, you still have tonight to go."

"It'll be alright," I said as I left.

The battalion was deployed on three hills. As on the previous day, I ruled against night bivouac, preferring to remain in our firing positions. Laor and Emmy remained at the foot of Tel Mar'i, ready to block any Syrian move. Two APCs of Lutsky's force were on the Tel. They had been there through the bombardment, serving as my eyes to spot any moves from the east. I was sorely tempted to call them down because they were completely exposed to heavy gunfire—I was afraid Lutsky's voice would fade from the radios at any moment. There was no room at the top for a tank platoon, but I decided this night to send two tanks up there, if only to make the APCs feel more secure; in any case they would be unable to use their guns because of their position. Anyway, the Syrians couldn't drive up there, because the only passable route was in our hands.

Half of Amnon's company and my tank were on Tel Fatma, and the other half on Tel a-Sarje. The gap between the two hills was closed off by three APCs—the doctor's, together with the battalion armorer and signals officer. They were guarding very well. They had more to fear than we, since they were not combatants.

Darkness fell fast. Laor and Emmy's tanks had succeeded in refueling in the last hours of daylight. The Syrians had discovered our supply point and dropped a salvo of Katyusha rockets on it. There was chaos, with rockets falling yards from the loaded trucks, but miraculously no one was hurt. Our enemy was now trying to be methodical, bringing down rocket salvoes every few minutes, but his fire, fortunately, was not accurate.

I had assigned Emmy and Laor a new artillery officer, who

had arrived from abroad to fight. I chose a good all-round view for myself, though I wasn't happy at being behind my two companies. Tel Mar'i gave us a 360-foot-high projection into Syrian territory with a commanding view of the surroundings. Tel Fatmah, where I was stationed, was 65 feet higher, though it wasn't noticeable from below. Both the hills were of major importance to our line around the bulge into Syria.

The battalion was in fine spirits, as the lighthearted chatter on the radio showed. Emmy and Laor were "arguing" about who had destroyed the most enemy tanks. These debates always ended with a reference to a suitcase that Laor had borrowed from Emmy. The owner claimed that Laor had no intention of returning it and that he wouldn't talk to him anymore over the radio until he got the bag back. Laor promised that after the war, he would give Emmy a snapshot of the case. But the time had come for my briefing.

" 'Policeman' stations, this is the battalion commander. I think we are going to have another tough night. The Syrians are yearning for Tel Mar'i. I believe they will try to take it tonight. As you know, efforts are being made to achieve a cease-fire here, as was done in the south—and that is the reason why this place has become an urgent matter for them."

I checked with the company commanders that they were all receiving me.

"I want all crew members awake till midnight. Don't hesitate to fire occasional machine-gun bursts as a precaution against infantry. The force on the Tel will maintain direct contact with me, and I want reports on any special problems that arise— direct reports. Those of you on the Tel must be particularly alert, both to defend yourselves and as the eyes of all of us. That's all."

I knew that we must spend the night in our positions, trying not to sustain last-minute injuries. No one apart from me knew that we were pulling out next day, but I gave in to the temptation of dropping a hint.

"This is the battalion commander. I want everyone to hear this. There will be a pleasant surprise for us tomorrow, but you'll only get the details then. Meanwhile, I wish us all a quiet night."

I was having visions of actually sleeping outside a tank.

"Battalion commander, Laor here. I understand that the surprise is a move farther east."

"Emmy here. You're going nowhere until you return my suitcase."

We settled down to wait for what the night would bring.

"Gideon, I'm hungry. Please prepare something," I asked.

"But we only ate two hours ago," Gideon mumbled as he scrambled out to get a ration pack from one of the storage compartments.

"I intend tonight to get back all the weight I've dropped from your lousy iron ration crackers during this war."

"Okay, okay, I'll find you some cookies."

The crew compartment suddenly filled up with all sorts of luxuries. My men were getting two or three parcels a day from home, and the place was beginning to look like a cross between a delicatessen and a bakery shop, with cigarette packs thrown in for luck. Apart from Yuval, none of us smoked, so we were waiting for an opportunity to get rid of the collection.

I had lost weight, and liked the idea. I smiled as I realized that the only system that worked for me was a war. Dieting never helped.

I was thinking about Nafah. We would be there for days, waiting on alert for any call to the line, so perhaps I would send my driver to bring Dalia and the children. I told the Headquarters company commander what to tell Haim, the driver, but in guarded terms because I didn't want anyone to spell out that we were moving out of the line next day. I was using the administrative frequency, to which few ears would be listening, and I told him to have Dalia and the kids brought to Degania Bet, where her sister lived. Minutes later he reported back that Haim knew what he had to do and had already gone.

At 2200 hours, there was tension on Emmy and Laor's sector. Laor reported figures moving in front of his tanks.

"Let them have a few bursts. You may not hit anything, but you'll rattle them," I said.

"I didn't see them. One of the tank commanders reported it."

"Take no risks. Fire the bursts."

I ordered Yehuda, the artillery officer, to drop a few star shells over the area. Then the Tel reported tank engines starting up to the east of us. The star shells illuminated the terrain, but there were no suspicious movements. We were tense and waiting, because the previous night Syrian infantry had approached to within 200 yards of the tanks, then fired bazooka rockets at first light. Laor's deputy had been wounded.

"I want a constant watch for tanks. I don't believe they'll move at night without infrared lights, but be prepared. Biber, can you still hear tanks?"

"Yes. I think they're two to three thousand yards from the Tel."

"Alright. You're probably exaggerating the distance, but stay listening. Yehuda, how are we off for star shells?"

"Fine. I don't think we'll be short. The problem is misfires, so I have to fire a large number."

His misfires were shells that did illuminate, but their parachutes didn't open—so the light they gave was almost useless.

"Emmy, Laor here. Have any of your men left their tanks?"

"No. All of mine are in their places," he replied somewhat icily.

How could Laor know that Emmy's company was not carrying out instructions?

"Right. I'm firing to the rear. Be prepared."

I watched the tracers but waited before asking Laor what was going on.

"I saw figures behind my tanks, and one of my commanders said that someone came up to the tank, took a look at it, then left."

I found it hard to believe, but we couldn't take chances. I asked Laor to tell the commander to get down and check his tank. Perhaps it had been sabotaged. Nothing was found, but the tension was still with us, and the reports of figures and of tank engines didn't stop. At least it helped me stay awake.

Towards dawn the miscellaneous noises stopped, and we waited to see what day would bring. At 0400 hours, as I lolled in my seat half-asleep, Gidi woke me to hear a news bulletin, but I only caught the last word: "Cease-fire."

"What did they say?"

"Syria has agreed to a cease-fire."

"Are you sure?"

"Sure. Sure. He said that the Syrian government had decided."

"Yanosh, Kahalani here."

"Yanosh here."

The response was immediate. I had expected having to wake him to pass on the good news.

"Did you hear the latest news bulletin?"

"No."

"The Syrians have decided to ask for a cease-fire."

"Are you sure?"

"Yes. We heard it on the radio a few minutes ago."

"That's really good news. Thanks."

He sounded as though something was troubling him. During the entire war, I hadn't heard him express any wish to see it end. That wouldn't have been his style, although I understood that he was tired of the war. We all were.

I passed the news on to all the company commanders but stressed that this was no reason to drop their guard. They asked whether this was the surprise I had promised, and I said no.

Dawn crept up on us slowly and in an unusual silence. No Syrian gunfire on our positions! The mystery of the night figures remained unsolved. The morning news bulletin announced a cease-fire for 1300 hours. By noon the commanders of the relief unit had come up to study the ground. Oded Erez, the battalion commander, came over for a chat. He told me that his battalion had been at Tel Fares when the war started.

"They came in hordes. We just couldn't stand up to them."

He sounded depressed about what had happened to his brigade. His battalion had suffered heavy casualties.

Oded tried to speed up his tanks, but they only began to arrive toward dark. We had to transfer the sectors commander by commander, as each new officer was briefed on his sector. The Syrians hadn't fired since morning. At 1300 hours, we climbed out of the tanks to stretch our legs and wash ourselves out of jerricans. Nevertheless, we still felt safer close to the tanks.

I didn't like moving on a dark night, over a rocky and twisting route. Emmy was ready to move, so he pulled back to Tel Fatma, where we waited for Laor. He completed his transfer of the sector in pitch dark, then pulled back in our direction.

"Is the route clear to you?" I asked Laor.

"Everything's clear, and I'm on my way to you. Incidentally, I'm towing one of the tanks. Apparently its engine is gone."

Some time passed, but he neither arrived nor did I hear tank engines. I asked him to blink a headlamp. He did so, but I couldn't see it.

"Are you absolutely certain of the way?"

"Yes. You can't see me because we're low down at the moment."

"Kahalani, Yanosh speaking. I want you to speed up your arrival here."

"Alright. Will be there immediately. Am organizing the force."

I didn't understand what Yanosh intended, unless he was following through on something said yesterday about silencing the terrorists in "Fatahland" to the north of Golan. They had been shelling the settlements along the Lebanese border.

Still no sign of Laor, though he insisted he would arrive any minute. I fired a green flare and asked whether he could see it. He confirmed, so I decided to wait a little longer. Finally he reported, "I have just reached the road."

"What road?"

There was no road between him and me. A quick glance at the map told me it had to be a road a few kilometers south of us.

"Stay where you are!"

"I've halted."

"I don't understand how you got there. I'm coming to get you. Be ready to indicate where you are."

"Kahalani, Yanosh here. I want you here personally as soon as possible."

He was obviously in a hurry, and I had to make a decision— whether to go to him directly or to get Laor out of his mess. Obviously, Laor had to come first. He had travelled south into territory the ownership of which wasn't clear, somewhere between our lines and theirs. South of us was the sector of Moshe "Musa" Peled's division.

"Brigade commander, Kahalani here. I must go get Laor."

"Give him a bearing and he'll arrive by himself."

"I'm asking to do it personally, otherwise it will take hours."

From the lack of response, I gathered that I was free to use my own judgment. We groped through the dark, between basalt rocks. Suddenly star shells lit the sky south of Laor. I guessed that the tension was rising, despite the cease-fire, because of tank movements. I called Yanosh to ask him to caution Peled's men not to open fire, and to stop lofting star shells. Why tell the Syrians that we were in a mess? I couldn't say I was happy that others now knew of navigation mistakes in my battalion, but we couldn't afford a tragedy.

I finally got to Laor to find that his tanks were stuck between giant basalt slabs inside a dried-up watercourse. A slightly abashed Laor climbed on my tank, and I gave him hell. It wasn't that he had made a mistake—but that he continued when he knew he was wrong. Together with him, I went down the line of tanks. One was indeed under tow, and two others had their bellies jammed onto basalt boulders, their tracks clear of the ground. We called the commanders together while I instructed those with serviceable vehicles on how to get the others out. Most of the attempts made before I arrived had resulted in damage to their towing cables, so two lengths were taken off my tank. Finally we were lined up in column facing northwest, ready to move. The way back was hard. Every mistake of mine meant that the column stopped, without any possibility of backing up because of the towed vehicles. We arrived at Tel Fatma, and Emmy and Amnon started down "America" road towards Nasaj. It was slow going. Amnon was in the lead, while Emmy brought up his own company, the sappers, and the APCs of the doctor and his entourage.

Yanosh was persistent. Again I guessed that he was planning a raid into Fatahland, and I was already thinking about how we would do it. He wanted me to hand over the column to one of the company commanders. With Laor's company on my heels, I reached the end of Emmy's column. They were on the road, trying to extricate a tank that had dropped into a pit, losing both tracks. I ordered the column to bypass the stranded tank and keep moving, but it wasn't long before they stopped again. This time a tank had stopped in a narrow pass, and there was no way to avoid it. Unable to use headlamps because of our proximity to the frontline, I crept up slowly to the stalled vehicle and supervised the efforts to tow it clear. Backing away from it, we dropped into a pit. I climbed down to find that my tracks were off the guide wheels. There was nothing to do but to board the armorer's APC and head for Yanosh, leaving my men to fix the tracks and get moving again. I ordered Amnon to bivouac.

"Do it the way you normally would, then set an order of priorities for solving the problems," I ordered.

Amnon was the senior and most experienced company commander. He would be able to cope, I knew.

"Brigade commander, Kahalani here, your location please?"

I was more or less where I expected to meet him. A pair of Jeep headlamps flickered 200 yards away. I guided the APC in alongside the Jeep, and was tense as I dropped off the vehicle. I had a revolver belt round my waist, field glasses hanging from my neck, a map and helmet in hand. I opened the Jeep door and was surprised to find Yanosh sitting alone at the wheel, while his driver sat next to the radio at the back.

"Shalom. What's going on? Where is everybody?"

"Get in. They've already gone in the direction of Nafah."

As we drove, I noted that the radios were tuned both to brigade and my battalion frequency, and the traffic was heavy. Yanosh had obviously been listening to my command channel, either from boredom or interest. He was driving fast, but I did not ask why.

"How are things in the battalion?"

Strange question if he had really been listening.

"I've never had such a lousy day. The tanks were getting stuck all over the place, as if they knew the war was over."

"Well, you were travelling without lights."

"What lights did you want me to use?"

"Infrared."

"From the start of this war, I've preferred not to use them."

"Never mind, it will be alright," he consoled me.

"Sure it will, but I have to put the battalion on its feet."

We were obviously circling around the subject.

"I heard you give Amnon the command. How is he?"

"Fine. But you're not telling me something."

"Kahalani ... I called you to tell you about ... a tragedy in your family. Your brother has been killed."

I choked and quaked.

"Which one?"

"Emanuel," he said, finally turning to face me. Tears flooded my eyes. The shock gave me a choking sensation. I remembered his sad eyes when last we parted. I envisioned him running, laughing, and finally the broad smile on his face the day he got married.

"He didn't even finish his honeymoon."

"Yes, I know. I remember the wedding."

"I always felt something would happen to him. . . ."

"Your parents have been waiting a long time for you. I want you to go home immediately."

"Home? But I've got to get the battalion back in shape. Who'll command?"

"Your gang is alright. They'll manage."

"When was he killed?"

"It's a few days since your parents called and asked that you come down, but I held up the message because I knew how important you were up there. And when I decided to tell you, Eitan was wounded."

"That's alright. Your decision was the correct one. I wouldn't have agreed to go."

I was recollecting having seen the brigade adjutant talking quietly with Yanosh and both of them glancing at me. I also remembered Gidi's anxiety about me that day; he was getting all my letters from home and withholding them. I guessed that the whole battalion knew about Emanuel, even though the news was kept from me. On a visit to brigade, I had heard that they had all called home from one of the field telephones. But when I tried, they told me the line was broken and they would let me know when it was fixed.

"Tell me, has your wife got any brothers in the army?"

"Yes. Two. Both in the regular army. Reuven, her twin, is in intelligence, and Ilan is a signals officer at Armor School."

"Dalia called today to say that one of them has fallen."

"What? Which one?"

"I don't know. I think it's the younger one, but I'm not sure."

"I don't understand. He only got married recently. His wife is pregnant—fifth month."

"Where do they live?"

"Kfar Warburg. That's two brothers she's lost. I don't know how her parents will take it."

"You go home and help them get over it. At the moment they're worried about you."

"I'll go, I hope the boys will manage without me."

The Jeep headed on towards Forward Position Seven and the Vale of Tears. As we crossed the frontier, Yanosh switched on his headlamps. To left and right of us were tanks and vehicles, Syrian and Israeli, abandoned at the roadside. As we passed close by the Vale of Tears, it finally hit me that I was really heading home—back to the place for which we had spilled so much blood. The Syrian tanks stood a silent memorial to the stubborn battle that had been fought here.

In the early hours of the morning, I left the base at Nafah, my head pillowed on the seat rest as Yanosh's car raced down the hills, heading for the coastal plain and home. . . .

31

THE LAST SALUTE

My Brothers the Heroes of Golan

I wanted to write to you, my brothers
With beards and sooty faces and all the other marks
I wanted to write to you—you who stood alone
Facing enemy tanks from front and flank.
You whose clanking tracks set a land trembling,
You who proved that armor is iron but man is steel,
To you, who gave a shoulder and extended a hand
And destroyed them in their masses one by one
I wanted to write you a hymn if only one
For each of the few who stood against the many.
I stand here on the ramps and count them by their scores
Sooty hulks and abandoned tanks and cold corpses
And I remember how you worked alone and in pairs
One turning on a light while the other struck from close,
And I look on towards the bloody path and Mazrat Beit Jan
And the night of move to ambush at America-Yair crossing
And the artillery that pounded at dawn,
And I remember the hundred and twenty-seven
And the gang on tanks, and their joy
When they heard and felt cease-fire coming.
I look back and see the faces of heroes,
Who will not come back with us, nor tell their exploits,
Those who saw the oncoming monster and fired till it stopped,
Who loaded another shell and another belt till they paid with their
    blood.
I remember all of them—Yair, Ami and Amir
Amir and Zelig Bluman and all the others who fought like lions till
    morning dawned.
I stand here alone and my heart is filled with a silent prayer: Let there
    be no more war . . .

—October 1973   Kobi

INDEX